"St. Francis de Sales is not only a supreme spiritual director; he is also a masterful writer. His classic writings are profound, practical, creative, and accessible to all. Deacon Matthew Newsome opens the treasure house of St. Francis de Sales's masterpiece with step-by-step suggestions, meditations, and Scripture passages. If you want to learn how to pray or deepen your prayer life, *The Devout Life* is a must-read."

—Fr. Dwight Longenecker
**Blogger, speaker, and author of *The Way of the Wilderness Warrior*, *Immortal Combat*, and *Beheading Hydra***

"What a blessing! Looking to live a holier life? Look no further. *The Devout Life* is the guidebook we all need: a beautifully crafted, accessible, inspiring companion to the classic work by St. Francis de Sales. Drawing on sources including Scripture, saints, contemporary writers, and, of course, St. Francis himself, Deacon Matthew Newsome gives us a new way of understanding that a life of holiness is available to all. It's like having your own personal spiritual director as close as your bookshelf. Packed with insight, wisdom, and a deeply prayerful approach, this is a book to return to again and again. I know I will—with gratitude and joy."

—Deacon Greg Kandra
Author of *A Deacon Prays*

"As a bishop, St. Francis De Sales labored tirelessly in the Lord's vineyard to cultivate the spiritual life of the lay faithful. How fitting it is that four centuries later, a deacon of the Church, whose calling it is to animate the devotion of all the baptized, has set about to make accessible again the fruits of this classic work. May this excellent 'introduction to the Introduction' serve the cause of Jesus Christ, living and reigning in a new generation of hearts!"

—Fr. Daniel G. Dozier
Byzantine Catholic priest and
author of 2C ʌ ‾ m

St. Francis de Sales

MAN
2022

Deacon Matthew Newsome

# The Devout Life
## A Modern Guide to Practical Holiness with St. Francis de Sales

SOPHIA INSTITUTE PRESS
Manchester, New Hampshire

Sophia Institute Press
Box 5284, Manchester, NH 03108
1-800-888-9344

www.SophiaInstitute.com

Sophia Institute Press® is a registered trademark of Sophia Institute.

paperback ISBN 978-1-64413-862-5

ebook ISBN 978-1-64413-863-2

Library of Congress Control Number: 2023930179

First printing

*To my wife, Joannie,*
*without whose inspiration*
*I would never have begun writing this book*
*and without whose encouragement*
*I would never have completed it*

# Contents

Part III

## Growing in Virtue

# Introduction

This is an introduction about an Introduction. St. Francis de Sales's masterpiece, *Philothea, or An Introduction to the Devout Life*, first published in 1609, remains one of the most popular spiritual guidebooks to this day. It ranks alongside St. Augustine's *Confessions*, Thomas à Kempis's *Imitation of Christ* and St. Teresa of Ávila's *Interior Castle* in terms of its enduring relevance for those seeking to grow in their relationship with God.

Why should a book about spiritual devotion written more than four hundred years ago remain so perennially popular? One reason is that St. Francis's *Introduction* was not primarily written for priests or cloistered religious but for the everyday Christian. In fact, St. Francis condemns the notion that true devotion is something attainable only by those with religious or clerical vocations.

"It is not merely an error but a heresy to suppose that a devout life is necessarily banished from the soldier's camp, the merchant's shop, the prince's court, or the domestic hearth," the saint writes. "Doubtless that form of devotion which is purely contemplative, monastic and religious, will not accord with their vocations, but there are other forms of devotion suitable to perfect a secular life" (1, 3).[1]

---

[1] Quotations from *An Introduction to the Devout Life* are generally taken from the English translation published by Joseph F. Wagner in 1923 and republished by TAN Books in 2010. I occasionally quote from the translations of Allan Ross (Burns, Oates, and

In an encyclical written on the three hundredth anniversary of his death, Pope Pius XI says that in *An Introduction to the Devout Life*, St. Francis "sets himself expressly to prove that holiness is perfectly possible in every state and condition of secular life."[2] The pope writes:

> It appears that Francis de Sales was given to the Church by God for a very special mission. His task was to give the lie to a prejudice which in his lifetime was deeply rooted and has not been destroyed even today, that the ideal of genuine sanctity held up for our imitation by the Church is impossible of attainment or, at best, is so difficult that it surpasses the capabilities of the great majority of the faithful and is, therefore, to be thought of as the exclusive possession of a few great souls.[3]

Being written for the layperson rather than the professed religious, *An Introduction to the Devout Life* is remarkably accessible. As a priest and later bishop of Geneva, St. Francis developed a reputation for preaching down-to-earth homilies, utilizing familiar imagery to illustrate complex spiritual principles to the common man. The same homey style comes through in his writing.

The content of St. Francis's *Introduction* is taken mainly from correspondence with his spiritual directees, chiefly one Madame Marie de Charmoisy, the wife of an ambassador who was cousin to St. Francis. It is presented as a collection of letters of instruction addressed broadly to *Philothea*, meaning "one who loves God." As

---

Washbourne, 1924) and John K. Ryan (Doubleday, 1950). These are referred to as the "Ross" and "Ryan" translations, respectively.

[2] Pope Pius XI, encyclical *Rerum Omnium Perturbationem* (January 26, 1923), no. 13.

[3] Ibid., no 4.

such, the *Introduction* consists of many short chapters, most only a page or two in length, making the content easy to digest for the average reader.

This present work is not a new translation of *An Introduction to the Devout Life*, nor is it a summary. Rather, it is intended to be a helpful resource, built upon the framework of St. Francis's *Introduction*, for anyone seeking to grow in devotion to God through individual or small-group study. My goal in writing it is to reintroduce the wisdom of the *Introduction* to a modern audience.

In his presentation of true devotion as something possible for all Christians, St. Francis de Sales anticipated by more than 350 years the universal call to holiness expressed by the Second Vatican Council. Moreover, the intervening centuries have given us the wisdom of many other saints. So imagine the *Introduction* as a road map that we'll be using as we journey to God. While we follow the route charted by St. Francis, we will pop in to visit a few other saintly friends along the way. I also draw from my fifteen years of experience as a college campus minister helping young adults appropriate the Catholic Faith and live as intentional disciples of Jesus Christ.

Each of the five sections in this book corresponds with a section from St. Francis's *Introduction to the Devout Life*. As the intention is for this book to be used for personal reflection or small-group discussion, each section is divided into brief chapters and concludes with reflection questions and a short Scripture passage for meditation. I recommend that readers take their time, reading no more than one chapter a day (or perhaps two or three while on retreat), allowing the spiritual lessons to sink in before they move on.

St. Francis de Sales often utilized imagery from the world around him to illustrate spiritual truths. In this, he is very much like our Lord, who taught using parables, drawing on familiar images to teach about heavenly realities. One of my favorite parables is that of the sower.

> A sower went out to sow. And as he sowed, some seed fell on the path, and birds came and ate it up. Some fell on rocky ground, where it had little soil. It sprang up at once because the soil was not deep, and when the sun rose it was scorched, and it withered for lack of roots. Some seed fell among thorns, and the thorns grew up and choked it. But some seed fell on rich soil, and produced fruit, a hundred or sixty or thirtyfold. Whoever has ears ought to hear. (Matt. 13:3–9)

The sower in this parable is God, and the seed is God's grace: the divine life that God wishes to plant in each one of us. That makes us the soil. Notice how in the parable, the sower scatters his seed indiscriminately, but not all of it bears fruit. What makes the difference is the quality of soil. If the seed falls on rocky ground, it won't take root. If it falls on parched soil, the plant will wither. If it falls among thorns, it will be choked out.

Practicing devotion to God is all about making our hearts fertile soil in which His seed of grace can be planted, nurtured, and brought to fruition. Although, to the best of my knowledge, St. Francis didn't intend this, it strikes me that the five sections of his *Introduction* correlate perfectly with this parable. Section 1 is all about preparing the soil for planting. If you've ever had a garden, you know it can involve hard work. You have to break up the soil to make it soft. You have to pull out any rocks you discover and uproot any weeds you find growing there. Preparing the soil is a laborious task, but it's necessary to do before you begin. This first section invites us to take a deep look into our hearts, to break up their rocky soil, and to make them ready to receive God's seed.

Section 2 is about planting that seed through prayer and participation in the sacraments. Section 3 deals with nourishing that seed and helping it to grow by practicing the virtues that will bear good fruit in our lives. But even as your garden grows, it needs tending to—not only by nourishing the good plants you want to grow there but by weeding out the plants that don't belong. Section 4 addresses how to weed out inevitable temptations before they bear their sinful fruit. Finally, every gardener knows you need to renew the soil from time to time to keep it fertile; and so the fifth and final section of this book contains guidance on making an annual "spiritual exam" so that God's seed may continue to bear in us the good fruit of holiness throughout our lives.

It will be wonderful if this study inspires people to read (or reread) *An Introduction to the Devout Life*. But above all, the purpose of this work is to help readers grow in the daily practice of devotion in such a way as to bring them closer to God through Christ and His Church. It's about making our souls fertile ground for grace. If my humble words prove even slightly helpful in this regard, it will have been well worth the effort to write this book. My hope is the same as that expressed by St. Francis de Sales himself in the introduction to the third edition of his work: "If God answers my prayers, you will put this little book to good use and receive great blessings from it."[4]

---

[4]  Ryan translation.

# About St. Francis de Sales

Francis de Sales was born in Savoie, France, on August 21, 1567, into a noble family. He was raised in the midst of the religious and social turmoil caused by the Protestant Reformation — nearby Geneva being a major stronghold of Calvinism. Pope Pius XI observes, "He seemed to have been sent especially by God to contend against the heresies begotten by the Reformation."[5] Initially educated by the Jesuits in Paris, Francis later studied civil and canon law at the University of Padua in Italy.

He was ordained a priest in 1593 and was named bishop of Geneva in 1602. Together with St. Jane Frances de Chantal, he founded the Order of the Visitation. In addition to *An Introduction to the Devout Life*, his other major works include *Treatise on the Love of God and Controversies*; the latter was originally written as a series of apologetical leaflets distributed by hand to explain and defend the Catholic religion against Protestant error to those who would not come to hear him preach.

Pius XI describes Francis as "a model of sanctity.... Endowed with every virtue, he excelled in meekness of heart, a virtue so peculiar to himself that it might be considered his most characteristic trait."[6] Far from being naturally meek, however, Francis was said to have had a short temper that he was able to conquer through

[5]  *Rerum Omnium Perturbationem*, no. 4.
[6]  Ibid., no. 6.

prayer, mortification of his will, and constant watchfulness over himself. "The meekness of St. Francis was therefore an effect of his tremendous will power, constantly strengthened by his lively faith and the fires of divine love which burned within him."[7]

He died on December 28, 1622. He was beatified in 1661 and was canonized in 1665 by Pope Alexander VII. In 1877, Pope Pius IX declared him to be a Doctor of the universal Church. He was named the patron saint of writers by Pope Pius XI in 1923. His feast is observed on January 24, the day of his burial at the Convent of the Visitation at Annecy.

[7]  Ibid., no. 10.

# St. Francis's Dedicatory Prayer

Ah, sweet Jesus, my Lord, my Savior, and my God, behold me here prostrate before your Majesty as I pledge and consecrate this work to your glory. By Your blessing give life to its words so that the souls for whom it has been written may receive from it the sacred inspirations I desire for them, in particular that of imploring your infinite mercy on my behalf to the end that while I point out to others the way to devotion in this world I myself may not be rejected and eternally condemned in the other, but that with them I may forever sing as a canticle of triumph words that with my whole heart I utter in witness of fidelity amid the hazards of this mortal life.

*Live, Jesus! Live, Jesus!*

Yes, Lord Jesus, live and reign in our hearts forever and ever. Amen.[8]

---

[8] Ryan translation.

Part I

# Preparing the Soil

*1*

# What Is Devotion?

Before embarking on our journey to devotion, we need to know what it is we are undertaking. If we don't know what we are seeking, how can we know when we've found it? It's a fair assumption that if you are reading this book, you are interested in growing closer to God through an intentional practice of the Christian faith. That's great! But what does that mean?

Let's begin with the word *devotion*. To have devotion is to have a strong love or loyalty to the object of devotion. Devotion happens when love meets enthusiasm. A fan of a sports team might catch highlights from their games on TV when he can. But a devoted fan never misses a game and is riveted to the screen every second—that is, when he's not attending the games in person, cheering the team on. All parents love their children, but when we think of devoted parents, we think of mothers and fathers who spend quality time with their kids, not from a sense of obligation but because they genuinely enjoy being with their children.

Consider these different ways a married person might describe his or her relationship with his or her spouse.

- I am faithful to my spouse.
- I am committed to my spouse.
- I am devoted to my spouse.

Each of these statements describes someone being true to his or her marital vows. But one might be faithful yet resentful; committed yet coldhearted. To be devoted, on the other hand, means not only being committed and faithful but being so gladly because loving one's spouse gives one joy—even when it involves suffering (more on that later).

Devotion to God is no different. In fact, the most common way the Scripture describes God's relationship with His people is as a marital relationship (see Eph. 5:21-32). To be devout means more than following God's commands from a sense of pious obedience. It means doing so eagerly from a sense of true love. Consider the Song of Solomon, the great love poem that is found in the center of the Bible, the very heart of the Scriptures. The bride (Israel, the Church) doesn't merely follow God out of obedience. She seeks Him out of love. "Let me seek him whom my soul loves." And when she finds him, she says, "I held him and would not let him go" (Song of Sol. 3:2, 4).

When you think of a devout Christian, you might think of a person who never misses daily Mass or who goes to Confession once a week. You might imagine an elderly widow clutching her rosary beads or a pious young mother sitting at the end of the pew with her head veiled and her polished children all in a row. You might picture a young man who continues altar serving well into adulthood, whom everyone says ought to consider the seminary. All these people seem very devout, and perhaps they are.

But St. Francis warns that appearances can be deceiving. "There are many counterfeits," he writes, "but only one true devotion." He explains:

> Everyone colors his devotion according to his tastes and inclinations. One is given to fasting, and whilst he fasts he holds himself to be devout, although his heart is full of bitterness.... Another would fain be devout because he daily

repeats many prayers, although, at the same time, he gives way to angry, proud and injurious language amongst his servants or associates. Another willingly opens his purse to give alms to the poor, but he cannot open his heart to forgive his enemies. . . . Thus many persons clothe themselves with a garb of external devotion, and the world believes them to be really devout and spiritual, whilst in truth they are mere statues or phantasms of devotion.[9]

St. Francis cautions us against equating a pious exterior with inner devotion so that we might not fall into the trap of thinking ourselves devout merely because we mimic the external trappings of devotion. We might fool the world that way. We might even fool ourselves. We will not fool God.

Devotion doesn't consist of doing pious things, good though they may be. Devotion means loving God, no more and no less. Just loving God may sound easy, but listen to how St. Francis describes it:

True and living devotion . . . is no other thing than a true love of God; yet not any kind of love; for, in so far as divine love beautifies our souls, and makes us pleasing to his divine Majesty, it is called grace; in so far as it gives us strength to do good, it is called charity; but when it reaches such a degree of perfection, that it makes us not only do good, but do so carefully, frequently and readily, then it is called devotion.[10]

By way of illustration, St. Francis offers a mundane comparison. Ostriches can't fly, he says. Fowls (chickens, turkeys, etc.) fly, but seldom and heavily, staying low to the ground. Eagles and doves fly high, fast, and often. Sinners, he says, are like ostriches, never flying to God.

[9]   Quotations in this chapter are taken from part 1, chapter 1.
[10]  Ross translation.

# The Devout Life

Good people who lack devotion are like fowl, flying only rarely and slowly to God by their good deeds, never getting very high. But devout souls are like eagles or doves. They don't just fly to God; they soar.

Devotion leads us to obey God's commands eagerly and with diligence. This is why St. Francis says, "Devotion consists in perfect charity [love]." This is the goal of the devout life—perfect love. Christ instructs us to "be perfect just as your heavenly Father is perfect" (Matt. 5:48). He's not telling us we have to be perfect athletes, artists, or academics (thank goodness). He's telling us to be perfect lovers.

So devotion is not about adopting a set of pious practices. It's about growing in holiness. To be holy means being like God, and God is love (1 John 4:8). The purpose of the devout life is to bring the image of God within us (see Gen. 1:27) to perfection by cooperating radically (down to the roots) with God's grace. The devout life is all about learning to love—God, one another, and ourselves—perfectly.

If that sounds intimidating (and perhaps even impossible), I have good news: God doesn't expect us to do it on our own. When Jesus spoke to His disciples about the demands of following Him, He said, "For human beings this is impossible, but for God all things are possible" (Matt. 19:26). All those who set out on this journey are promised every necessary heavenly aid.

Are you ready to begin?

*Questions for Reflection*

1. What things other than God are you devoted to (family, work, hobbies, etc.)? Are any of these things obstacles to devotion to God?

2. What external practices (e.g., the Rosary, Adoration, Bible studies, other prayers, fasting) have you found helpful in growing in your relationship with God? Have you engaged in pious practices merely externally out of a sense of obligation? What, if anything, has been their fruit?

3. Does the "perfect charity" St. Francis describes seem possible to you? If not, what are the obstacles to attaining it? What graces from God do you need to overcome those obstacles?

*Scripture for Meditation*

Blessed those whose way is blameless,
who walk by the law of the LORD.
Blessed those who keep his testimonies,
who seek him with all their heart.
They do no wrong;
they walk in his ways.
You have given them the command
to observe your precepts with care.
May my ways be firm
in the observance of your statutes!
Then I will not be ashamed
to ponder all your commandments.
I will praise you with sincere heart
as I study your righteous judgments.
I will observe your statutes;
do not leave me all alone. (Ps. 119:1–8)

## 2

# A Joyful Burden

Living a devout life—seeking to grow in holiness, to become more like God, and to give yourself more perfectly in love—sounds like hard work. And it can be difficult, especially at first. Like anything else worthwhile, it takes effort and diligence. It's important to recognize that it can at times feel like a burden; but the secret of devotion is that it makes our burdens light and even sweet!

St. Francis warns those embarking on the path of devotion that the world likes to "calumniate holy devotion, representing devout persons with a gloomy, sad and irritable countenance."[11] The world imagines that living a devout Christian life means forsaking all joy and pleasure, walking around with our heads bowed and hands folded in pious penitential prayer—a perpetual Lenten fast with never an Easter feast. Or as Mr. Tumnus described Narnia under the curse of the White Witch, "always winter and never Christmas."[12]

There is no love without sacrifice, and sacrifice is hard. There's no way around that reality. Even God, in expressing His love for us, had to suffer and die on the Cross; and He tells those of us who would love Him in return that we must take up our own crosses *daily* and follow Him (Luke 9:23). That means denying our wants and desires much of the time. Love requires us to do violence to our ego, and so we naturally resist its demands. For this reason,

---

[11] Quotations in this chapter are taken from part 1, chapter 2.
[12] C. S. Lewis, *The Lion, the Witch and the Wardrobe*, chap. 2.

many people—even lifelong Christians—never really set out to live a life of devotion. G. K. Chesterton once remarked, "The Christian ideal has not been tried and found wanting. It has been found difficult; and left untried."[13]

But if we want to know whether living a devout life is worth the struggle, we shouldn't listen to those who dismiss it as too demanding and so never try. We should listen instead to those who actually lived lives of intentional Christian discipleship. We should listen to the saint and ask them whether the sacrifice involved in living a devout life was worth it.

To read the life of any saint is to discover a life infused with joy—even those saints who suffered greatly. And none suffered more greatly than the martyrs. The most remarkable thing we discover in the account of the early Christian martyrs is their great joy even amid torture and death. The way the Christian martyrs met death—not only with dignity but with joy—astounded the pagan onlookers. As the author of *The Martyrdom of St. Polycarp* (second century) observed, "All the people wondered that there should be such a difference between the unbelievers and the elect."[14] The joyful witness of the martyrs (the word *martyr* means "witness") is what caused the Church to grow so rapidly even as the Roman Empire fought so hard to suppress it. This truth was attested to by Tertullian when he remarked at the end of the second century that "the blood of the martyrs is the seed of the Church."[15]

Most of us (hopefully) will not have to suffer such violent persecution for our faith. But as St. Francis de Sales observes, "If devotion can soften torture and death itself, can it not lighten

---

[13] G. K. Chesterton, *What's Wrong with the World*, chap. 5.

[14] *The Martyrdom of Polycarp* 16.

[15] Tertullian, *Apologeticus* 50.

the daily path of duty?" This is what the naysayers of the world don't understand about devotion. It can make suffering sweet. St. Francis compares devotion to a bee that takes bitter pollen and turns it into sweet honey. The world sees only the bitterness of fasting, prayer, mortification, almsgiving, and self-restraint. "But the world does not see the internal, hearty devotion which renders all such actions easy, pleasant, and grateful."

Having an internal attitude of devotion not only makes hardship more bearable; it also has a tempering effect on good fortune. We might not think good things need tempering, but tempering even licit pleasures teaches us not to place too high a value on them. Devotion allows us to accept good things with grace, being grateful for the good that they are without mistaking them for the highest good. Devotion prevents us from valuing the gift over the Giver. Therefore, St. Francis says devotion "draws some good alike from honor and contempt, it accepts both joy and suffering with an even spirit, and fills us with a marvelous sweetness."

At the end of his letter to the Philippians, St. Paul encourages the Christians of that city to continue living the way of devotion he taught them:

> Finally, brothers, whatever is true, whatever is honorable, whatever is just, whatever is pure, whatever is lovely, whatever is gracious, if there is any excellence and if there is anything worthy of praise, think about these things. Keep on doing what you have learned and received and heard and seen in me.…
>
> I know indeed how to live in humble circumstances; I know also how to live with abundance. In every circumstance and in all things I have learned the secret of being well fed and of going hungry, of living in abundance and

of being in need. I have the strength for everything through him who empowers me. (Phil. 4:8–9, 12–13)

Following God's commands and living a devout Christian life can at times be difficult, because love is difficult. Self-denial is difficult. Subjecting your will to a higher authority is difficult.

Jesus tells those who would follow Him, "Take my yoke upon you" (Matt. 11:29). A yoke is a wooden frame fitted over the shoulders of two oxen, binding them to each other, forcing them to work together as they follow the direction of the plowman. Christ is saying that we need to be yoked to Him, in order to work in tandem with Him to follow the Father's will. To wear a yoke is a burden. But unlike the farmer's yoke, Christ tells us, "my yoke is easy, and my burden light" (Matt. 11:30).

*Questions for Reflection*

1. What kinds of sacrifices do you make for your loved ones? What kinds of sacrifices do you make for God?
2. In what ways does God help you with your burdens?
3. Why would good fortune be something that needs to be tempered? What does it mean for you to temper the joy that comes from good things?

*Scripture for Meditation*

Come to me, all you who labor and are burdened, and I will give you rest. Take my yoke upon you and learn from me, for I am meek and humble of heart; and you will find rest for yourselves. For my yoke is easy, and my burden light. (Matt. 11:28–30)

3

# Devotion Is for Everyone

Everybody wants to get to Heaven. But what is Heaven? Most people today view Heaven as the ultimate reward God gives to "good people" when they die—perfect and eternal happiness, whatever that might be. But our Faith teaches us that Heaven is not so much a reward as a relationship. *The Catechism of the Catholic Church* (CCC) tells us that is the "perfect life with the Most Holy Trinity" in which "the blessed continue joyfully to fulfill God's will" (1024, 1029). If Heaven is eternal union with God, it follows that we must *want* to be in union with Him; otherwise we won't be happy there.

St. John Henry Newman preached a sermon on the necessity of holiness in this life for happiness in the next. He said, "Heaven is not a place of happiness *except* to the holy.... Heaven would be hell to an irreligious man."[16]

This is why the cultivation of devotion in this life is so important. We might imagine that since everyone wants to go to Heaven, everyone would also want to foster devotion to God, since that's what Heaven is all about. Yet there is a tendency, even among Christians, to assume that religious devotion is mainly for priests, nuns, and monks—the professional religious class who have a special interest in that sort of thing. For the rest of us, it's enough that we go to church on Sundays and say a few prayers now and again.

[16] St. John Henry Newman, "Holiness Necessary for Future Blessedness," in *Parochial and Plain Sermons*.

The false assumption that pious devotion is only for the chosen few in the Church is not a new problem. More than sixteen hundred years ago, St. Augustine reminded his flock that the call of discipleship "is not a command for virgins to obey and brides to ignore, for widows and not for married women, for monks and not for married men, or for the clergy and not for the laity. No, the whole Church, the entire body, all the members in their distinct and varied functions, must follow Christ."[17]

In our own age, the Second Vatican Council (1962–1965) reminds us that "all in the Church … have a vocation to holiness."

> All of Christ's faithful, no matter what their rank or station, have a vocation to the fullness of the Christian life and the perfection of charity…. They must follow Christ's footsteps, be moulded to his likeness, be attentive to the will of the Father in all things, be whole-heartedly devoted to the glory of God and the service of their neighbour. This is the way in which an abundant harvest will grow from the holiness of God's People.[18]

Far from being a novel teaching of the 1960s, the universal call to holiness belongs to the apostolic foundation of the Church. "This is the will of God; your holiness" (1 Thess. 4:3).

So we shouldn't be surprised to find St. Francis de Sales reminding Christians in his time of this truth. With his usual penchant for agricultural metaphor, he observes that just as God made all sorts of plants, each to bear fruit of its own kind, "He commands Christians, who are the living plants of His Church,

---

[17] St. Augustine, *Sermon 46*, 9.

[18] Second Vatican Council, Dogmatic Constitution on the Church *Lumen Gentium* (LG) (November 21, 1964), no. 39, 40.

to bring forth the fruits of devotion, each according to his calling and vocation."

The Second Vatican Council calls the fruit of devotion a "harvest of grace." Just as different varieties of plants bear different fruit, each proper to its nature, the harvest of grace "has many different forms of expression among individuals."[19] St. Francis writes:

> There is a different practice of devotion for the gentleman and the mechanic; for the prince and the servant; for the wife, the maiden, and the widow; and still further, the practice of devotion must be adapted to the capabilities, the engagements, and the duties of each individual.[20]

In other words, while the object of devotion is the same for everyone (holiness), the form and expression of devotion differ not only according to each individual's vocation and state in life but also according to the individual's natural disposition, gifts, and circumstances.

The life of a celibate monk is supposed to be different from the life of a family man. If it isn't, something is wrong. The demands of being the pastor of a parish are different from the demands of being a stay-at-home mother or a career professional. The circumstances of an elderly widow are different from the circumstances of a college freshman. Yet all are called to holiness.

The entire Church is called to follow Christ, but the entire Church is not called to monasticism, marriage, or missionary life. The Church is united as the Body of Christ, but a body is made up of many different parts. As St. Paul points out to the Christians of his day in Corinth, "If an ear should say, 'Because I am

---

[19]  LG 39.
[20]  Quotations in this chapter are taken from part 1, chapter 3.

not an eye I do not belong to the body,' it does not for this reason belong any less to the body. If the whole body were an eye, where would the hearing be?... As it is, God placed the parts, each one of them, in the body as he intended" (1 Cor. 12:16–18). In our devotional practices, we must consider what is proper to our state and disposition (and what is foreign to it).

The married father of six is not called to pray like a monk. When one of my sons was an infant, I confessed to my pastor that my prayer life was not all it should be. "I get up early to pray," I told him, "but lately the baby hasn't been sleeping well. I'll just be getting started, and he'll wake up crying. I go get him so my wife can sleep in, since she's been up all night with feedings. I change his diaper, then try to get back to prayer with the baby in my arms. That's when he throws up on me. And as I'm cleaning up that mess, the older kids wake up and start asking me for juice and breakfast. By the time I sit down to pray again, I have to rush so I can get to work on time."

My pastor just smiled and offered me an important reminder. "You are not a monk. You are a husband and father with small children and a full-time job. That's your state in life, and that's where you are called to pray from. It might not *feel* like good prayer to you, but we don't pray to make ourselves feel good. We pray to let God know we love Him and want to do His will. And His will for you is to be a good husband and father. That's how you are meant to serve Him. The fact that you are praying even when you don't feel like you're getting anything out of it just shows that you are doing it for God, not yourself. God honors that kind of prayer."

A husband cannot have the devotional life of a monk without neglecting his family. A monk cannot have the active apostolate of a missionary without doing damage to his monastic calling. A pastor cannot live the life of a hermit without abandoning his flock to the wolves. We are all called to devotion, but each in our own way.

Our individual vocations and circumstances are the particular means God gives us to grow in holiness, if we accept them as such and choose to cooperate with His grace.[21] Rather than thinking of our vocation or state in life as obstacles to devotion, we should look on devotion as the surest means to perfect our vocation.

St. Francis de Sales observes, "True devotion does us no harm whatsoever, but instead perfects all things. When it goes contrary to a man's lawful vocation, it is undoubtedly false."[22] He points out:

> Every vocation becomes more agreeable when united with devotion. Care of one's family is rendered more peaceable, love of husband and wife more sincere, service of one's prince more faithful, and every type of employment more pleasant and agreeable.[23]

When a priest grows in devotion, it makes him a better priest. When a nun grows in devotion, it makes her a better nun. When married people grow in devotion, it makes them better husbands, wives, and parents. When students practice devotion, it makes them better students. No matter our state in life, cultivating devotion will allow us to flourish in whatever field God has planted us in.

As proof that true devotion is possible for everyone, we need only look at the many and varied examples of the saints. St. Monica was the mother of a rebellious son and the wife of a pagan. St. Thomas Aquinas was a scholar who spent his life in the university. St. John of the Cross was a contemplative monk. St. Margaret

---

[21] LG 41.

[22] Ryan translation.

[23] Ibid.

of Scotland was a queen and mother of eight children. St. John Vianney was a parish priest. Bl. Pier Giorgio Frassati was a college student and outdoor enthusiast. St. Elizabeth Ann Seton was a widow who founded a religious order. St. José Luis Sánchez del Rio was a fourteen-year-old boy who bravely accepted execution during the Mexican Cristero War rather than to deny Christ.

Regardless of age, income, occupation, or education, each and every one of us is called to holiness. A devout life is possible for us all. "His divine power has bestowed on us everything that makes for life and devotion, through the knowledge of him who called us by his own glory and power" (2 Pet. 1:3).

## Questions for Reflection

1. What is your vocation or state in life? What obligations and responsibilities are inherent to it? What opportunities does it provide for devotion?
2. Have you ever felt that the limitations inherent in your state in life were obstacles to pursuing devotion?
3. How might growing in your devotion to God benefit your vocation?

## Scripture for Meditation

Now you are Christ's body, and individually parts of it. Some people God has designated in the church to be, first, apostles; second, prophets; third, teachers; then, mighty deeds; then, gifts of healing, assistance, administration, and varieties of tongues. Are all apostles? Are all prophets? Are all teachers? Do all work mighty deeds? Do all have gifts of healing? Do all speak in tongues? Do all interpret? Strive eagerly for the greatest spiritual gifts. (1 Cor. 12:27–31)

4

# Finding a Guide

The Acts of the Apostles tells of an encounter between the deacon Philip and a eunuch from Ethiopia. Philip saw the eunuch seated in his chariot and reading a scroll of the prophet Isaiah. Philip asked him, "Do you understand what you are reading?" The eunuch replied, "How can I, unless someone instructs me?" So Philip joined him in his chariot and "proclaimed Jesus to him" (8:26–39).

The best way to grow in knowledge is to have a good teacher. The best way to travel in a new country is to have a guide who has been there before. Our spiritual journey is no different. "Do you seriously wish to travel the road to devotion?" St. Francis de Sales asks. "If so, look for a good man to guide and lead you."[24]

From the earliest days of the Church, those seeking to become more devout have sought out teachers in the Faith as guides and spiritual fathers. This makes sense on a practical level in terms of learning from a knowledgeable teacher. But a major element of spiritual growth is learning to put our egos on the back burner and conform our desires to God's will. In other words, we have to learn obedience. If we are trying to do that on our own, it's all too easy to fall into the trap of mistaking what *we* want for what God wants for us. Self-direction is rarely fruitful for that reason.

---

[24] Ryan translation. Quotations in this chapter are taken from part 1, chapter 4.

So St. Francis says, "You will never so safely find the will of God as in the path of humble obedience."

An objective third party can see our spiritual blind spots. A wise director can identify areas of weakness—and strength—that we may be unaware of in ourselves. He or she can help us perceive how God is working in our lives in ways that we might not have considered. For these and many other reasons, having a good spiritual director is invaluable for anyone seeking to become devout.

What does spiritual direction involve? In some ways, it's like going to Confession, without sacramental absolution. Like Confession, it should be confidential, so we can feel free to discuss our sins and struggles. But it is not simply confessing our sins; spiritual direction provides a greater opportunity to examine the circumstances and motivating factors of our sins; to probe beneath the surface and identify root causes and habitual patterns of behavior.

Beyond helping us overcome vice and grow in virtue (which is a fundamental aspect of devotion), spiritual direction can also help us discern how God is calling us to serve Him in our vocations and to better love Him and love our neighbors. As we face major decisions or experience spiritual hardship, spiritual direction can help us better understand how God is at work in our lives.

A spiritual director is *not* your therapist or life coach. Spiritual direction is not the place to "get your life together" or tackle all your psychological issues. It's an opportunity to dig deep into your soul, accompanied by a trusted guide, to discover how God is calling you to respond to His grace. St. Francis instructs us to "have towards [your director] an open heart in all faithfulness and sincerity, laying bare to him alike your evil and your good without pretense or dissimulation. By this means what is good in you will be examined and established; what is evil remedied and corrected."

Finding an appropriate director can be a challenge. St. Francis even admits that "there are few suited to such an office. He must be filled with charity, knowledge, and discretion." A spiritual director does not necessarily need to be a priest, but members of the clergy and professed religious men and women are more likely to have the theological and spiritual formation required to offer good direction.

There is no certifying body for spiritual directors, although there are schools that offer training. Some of these offer good, solid Catholic formation, but others take more of a New Age approach to spiritual direction (sometimes erroneously labeled as "Catholic"). So just because someone is a "certified spiritual director," that does not mean that that person would make a good choice. In general, good spiritual directors do not need to advertise their services. The Holy Spirit brings them people who need their guidance.

It may take a while to find a spiritual director. Ask for recommendations from your pastor or local clergy (who should all be receiving spiritual direction themselves). And remember: just because a particular director works well for one person does not mean he or she will work well for you. You will most likely need to meet with a spiritual director a few times to determine whether that person will offer the direction you need to grow in devotion.

Pray and be patient. St. Francis tells us that "since it is so all-important for you to begin this holy course of devotion led by a safe guide, if you heartily pray that God would give you such, he will supply your need in his own way."

In the meantime, allow yourself to be guided by the spiritual masters of the past. The writings of saints are considered classics precisely because their usefulness as spiritual guides has been proven by the test of time. They can be sure and certain teachers if we approach them with humility and a desire to learn (and be changed by) the wisdom they offer.

And do not neglect the spiritual direction that is available in the confessional! Even though the object of confession is the sacramental absolution of sins and not spiritual guidance per se, the advice offered in confession can be of great help to those who have no access to direction otherwise. Seventeenth-century Carmelite monk Br. Lawrence of the Resurrection admitted that "as he knew his obligation to love God in all things … he had no need of a director to advise him, but that he needed very much a confessor to absolve him."[25]

---

[25] Lawrence of the Resurrection, *The Practice of the Presence of God* (Grand Rapids: Spire Books, 1967), second conversation.

## Questions for Reflection

1. What aspects of your spiritual life do you think would benefit most from spiritual direction?
2. Which people in your parish, school, diocese, or community might you approach for spiritual direction?
3. What spiritual writers, either contemporary or from the history of the Church, have you found to be helpful spiritual guides?

## Scripture for Meditation

Faithful friends are a sturdy shelter; whoever finds one finds a treasure.

Faithful friends are beyond price; no amount can balance their worth.

Faithful friends are life-saving medicine; those who fear God will find them. (Sir. 6:14–16)

# 5

# Purifying the Soul

Resurrection is always preceded by death. Before we can become a new creation, we must die to our former self. This is the significance of Baptism. The waters of Baptism represent the life-giving spring flowing from the Temple of the New Israel (Ezek. 47:1–12), but they also represent the destructive waters of the flood in the days of Noah (Gen. 6:9–9:17). Baptism is a rebirth because it is also a burial.

But spiritual purification is not a one-and-done deal. This is why even after Baptism, we continue to struggle against sin. St. Francis de Sales points out that while some saints experience perfect purification in a single moment, these are the exception to the norm. "Ordinary purification and healing," he says, "whether of body or soul, are accomplished by little and little, progressing slowly and often hardly at all."[26] Purification is a process, and we should expect it to take time. Even St. Paul, whom St. Francis holds up as an example of miraculous purification, still says years after his conversion, "I do not do the good I want, but I do the evil I do not want" (Rom. 7:19). How many of us can relate to that feeling?

Spiritual purification involves not just repenting of sin but repenting of attachment to sin. This is an ongoing process of conversion that, for most of us, is the work of a lifetime. St. Francis encourages us to "be patient and courageous" as we

---

[26] Quotations in this chapter are taken from part 1, chapter 5.

progress and warns against two mistakes we can easily fall into. The first is becoming frustrated with the slowness of our progress. When we keep falling back into habitual sin despite our efforts to do God's will, we can easily become discouraged and be tempted to give up altogether on the practice of devotion. The second mistake is to yield to the opposite temptation and believe we've made so much spiritual progress that we are now immune to sin. St. Francis warns that souls who make this second mistake are in danger of a spiritual relapse, as they "regard themselves as perfect before they have scarcely begun, and try to fly without wings."[27]

We can expect the process of purification to be a struggle, and there will likely be one or two sins we struggle with especially. This is normal. One parishioner expressed frustration to his pastor because he found himself confessing the same sin over and over again. Far from being concerned, his pastor replied, "Do you think it would be better if you had a new sin to confess every time?"

We are spiritually weak in certain areas more than others, and it is precisely in these areas that the devil attacks us. The devil is a smart tactician. He knows where our defenses are weak, and that's where he concentrates his efforts and tempts us the most. The trick is not to give up! Our victory lies in the struggle. As long as we struggle against sin, we are still in the fight. The only way to lose is to quit. "Victory does not lie in ignoring our infirmities, but in resisting them."

St. Francis reminds us that "being grieved by [our sins] is not consenting to them—our humility is at times tested by the wounds which we receive in this spiritual combat, but we are never conquered unless we lose our courage or our life.... It is

---

[27] Ryan translation.

a favorable feature of this war, that so long as we will fight, we must be victorious."

Frequent confession is a powerful weapon in this spiritual combat. The *Catechism* reminds us that even after "the new birth of Baptism" there is "the struggle of *conversion* directed toward holiness and eternal life to which the Lord never ceases to call us" (1426). This is why "Christ instituted the sacrament of Penance [Confession] for all sinful members of his Church; above all for those who, since Baptism, have fallen into grave sin" (1446).

As powerful a weapon as it is, far too few people make good use of it. St. Francis de Sales laments that many people's confessions "are full of faults" because they make little or no preparation and lack true contrition. They "therefore confess with a tacit intention of repeating their sins, since they will neither avoid the occasion of falling, nor take the needful steps for amending their lives."

For sacramental Confession to be valid, the penitent must have contrition, defined by the Council of Trent as "sorrow of the soul and detestation for the sin committed, together with the resolution not to sin again."[28] The requirement of "resolution not to sin again" can sometimes lead people to become frustrated and even discouraged, especially if they have a tendency to scrupulosity. It is very important to remember that resolving not to sin again does not mean being free from all temptation or concupiscence (the tendency to sin that is the result of the Fall) (CCC 1426). It means having a *desire* to be free from sin, even if we know—and accept—that freedom will involve a long healing process.

There is a difference between saying, "I have an attachment to this sin and I know I am likely to repeat it, but with God's grace

---

[28]  Quoted in CCC 1451.

I want to work to be free of it," and saying, "I have an attachment to this sin and I know I am going to repeat it, so I've accepted it as part of who I am." The former is contrition. The latter is not. It is precisely those who struggle with an inclination to a particular sin who stand to benefit the most from frequent Confession. Never allow lingering attachment to sin to keep you from Confession, as you would not allow a lingering illness to keep you from seeing a doctor!

The kind of purification St. Francis de Sales wants to lead us to (and that God wants for us) is not simply freedom from sin but freedom from the *affection* for sin. Avoiding sin while maintaining affection for sin, the saint writes, is "like sick men abstaining from melons. They don't eat them solely because the doctor warns them that they'll die if they do, but they begrudge giving them up, talk about them, would eat them if they could, want to smell them at least, and envy those who can eat them." Many penitents, even while avoiding sin, "would like very much to commit sins if they could do so without being damned."

This only means we have come to fear the punishment for sin. To be truly devout, we must cleanse our hearts of all attachment to sin; to hate sin "with a hearty, vigorous contrition" and detest "not only the sin itself, but every affection, circumstance, and inducement which tends towards it." To help turn our hearts away from love of sin, St. Francis recommends that we begin our quest for devotion by making a general confession.

A general confession is a devotional confession not just of the sins we have committed since our last confession but of all the sins of our past life. It should be made to a good confessor after a thorough and prayerful examination of conscience, with full knowledge that by our sins we have lost God's grace, forfeited Heaven, merited Hell, and renounced the love of God, yet with full hope and trust in God's mercy. St. Francis recommends a general confession because it

> increases our self-knowledge, incites a healthy sorrow for our past sins, fills us with admiration of the patience and mercy of God, calms our heart, relieves our mind, excites in us good resolutions, enables our spiritual Father to guide us more certainly, and opens our hearts to speak fully and with confidence in our future confessions.

To prepare us to make a general confession, St. Francis offers a series of meditations, which we will cover in the following chapter. He suggests that we make one of these meditations per day, preferably in the morning so that we can "ruminate over it during the rest of the day."

## Questions for Reflection

1. Do you think you go to Confession often enough? If not, what prevents you from going more often? What steps could you take to go more often?
2. For personal reflection: What sins are you especially attached to? What can you do to avoid the occasions of those sins?
3. For group discussion: What does the "resolution not to sin again" mean to you in practice? What do you imagine freedom from attachment to sin to be like?

## Scripture for Meditation

Have mercy on me, God, in accord with your
  merciful love;
in your abundant compassion blot out my
  transgressions.
Thoroughly wash away my guilt;
and from my sin cleanse me.
For I know my transgressions;
my sin is always before me.
Against you, you alone have I sinned;
I have done what is evil in your eyes
So that you are just in your word,
and without reproach in your judgment.
Behold, I was born in guilt,
in sin my mother conceived me.
Behold, you desire true sincerity;
and secretly you teach me wisdom.

Cleanse me with hyssop, that I may be pure;
wash me, and I will be whiter than snow.
You will let me hear gladness and joy;
the bones you have crushed will rejoice.
Turn away your face from my sins;
blot out all my iniquities.
A clean heart create for me, God;
renew within me a steadfast spirit. (Ps. 51:2–12)

# 6

# Meditations

In this chapter, we offer a series of ten meditations recommended by St. Francis de Sales to help us prepare for a general confession.

We begin each day's meditation by placing ourselves in the presence of God. What does that mean? Aren't we always in the presence of God? Certainly we are. But we are not always aware of that presence. Increasing awareness of God's presence in our lives is what prayer is all about.

St. John of Damascus defines prayer as "the raising of one's mind and heart to God."[29] The mind is the seat of our intellect, and the heart is traditionally considered to be the seat of our will. These two aspects of our being, our rational intellect and free will, are what make us "in the image and likeness of God" (Gen. 1:27): they separate us from the lower animals. To raise one's mind and heart to God, then, is to orient the divine aspects of our being to their origin and proper end. That is why we were given intellect and will to begin with; so that we might *know* and *love* God.

We can think about and desire God at any time, whether at Mass, while praying the Rosary, while driving to work, or while washing the dishes. This is why St. Paul's instruction

---

[29] Quoted in CCC 2559.

to "pray without ceasing" is not unreasonable (1 Thess. 5:17). But ever since the Fall, this has not been our natural disposition. "We do not know how to pray as we ought, but the Spirit itself intercedes with inexpressible groanings" (Rom. 8:26). We need the Holy Spirit's help, and we need to cooperate with the work of the Spirit to establish a discipline of prayer. Creating a habit of prayer at specific times is how we learn to maintain a prayerful disposition at all times.

To place yourself in the presence of God involves a quieting of your spirit. It involves recalling your heart and mind back from whatever else might be occupying them, to remind them that God exists and that He loves you and wants to be loved by you. Nothing else matters more than this truth.

Most of us are creatures of habit, so to set yourself up for success, it helps to have a regular routine. As much as you are able, try to make your daily meditation at the same time each day (St. Francis de Sales recommends early morning) and in the same place. Establish a ritual. Light a candle. Make the Sign of the Cross. Having a routine helps your body and mind "get into prayer mode" more easily.

Most of us are easily distracted, so I recommend having close by a sacred image, such as a crucifix or an icon of Christ, for your eyes to focus on. This will help bring your mind back to prayer when it begins to wander. When it does wander, don't become frustrated. Just refocus your thoughts on God and continue your meditation.

Once you have settled yourself in the place where you will be praying, take a moment before you begin to focus your thoughts on God. Then invite the Holy Spirit to inspire you, and ask your guardian angel to intercede for you as you begin your meditation.

At the end of each meditation, St. Francis de Sales asks us to "make a little spiritual nosegay." *Nosegay* is somewhat of an archaic term, often translated as "bouquet." This does not do justice to the image St. Francis means to invoke. We think of a bouquet as an arrangement of flowers kept in a vase to brighten up a room in our home. This is not what a nosegay is. A nosegay was meant to be carried with you. It was a small bouquet of fragrant flowers that people of St. Francis's time would carry or wear pinned to their clothing for visual and aromatic pleasure. By asking us to make a spiritual nosegay, St. Francis wants us to apply this same concept to prayer. He explains this in a later part of his *Introduction to the Devout Life*:

> Those who have been walking in a beautiful garden do not leave it willingly without taking away with them four or five flowers, in order to inhale their perfume and carry them about during the day: even so, when we have considered some mystery in meditation, we should choose one or two or three points in which we have found most relish, and which are specially proper to our advancement, in order to remember them throughout the day, and to inhale their perfume spiritually.[30]

My preferred means of doing this is by using a prayer journal. This is a small notebook in which I can quickly jot down short passages of Scripture or particular words or images that come to me in my meditation. These, then, form the basis of my spiritual nosegay for the day. Even though I rarely go back to read what I wrote, I find that the mere act of writing these things down allows me to carry them in my memory such that, when prompted by my angel, they spring to the forefront of my thoughts as I go about my daily business.

[30] Pt. 2, chap. 7, Ross translation.

By instructing us to make a spiritual nosegay, St. Francis wants us to carry the "sweet aroma" of our prayer with us throughout the day. God is always with us, whether we are aware of Him or not, but we need frequent reminders of His presence. A key aspect of living a devout life is maintaining a conscious awareness of the presence of God. Beginning each day with a time of prayer, and then carrying the fruits of that prayer with us as we go about the day's business is essential to this process.

*Suggestion:* St. Francis envisions us making these ten meditations, one per day. If you are doing this exercise as part of a weekly prayer group, however, you may find it expedient to do two meditations on certain days to fit them all within one week. In this case I suggest combining meditations 1 and 2 (Creation and Purpose), 7 and 8 (Hell and Heaven), and 9 and 10 (Choice and Devotion). When making two meditations on the same day, I suggest doing them as far apart as possible (one in the morning and one in the evening) in order not to rush through either one. An alternative would be to do five meditations per week over a two-week period.

## Questions for Reflection

1. What time of day would be best for your meditation? Don't consider only what time would be most convenient but what time would be most conducive to thoughtful prayer. Are you a morning person or a night person? When are you most alert?

2. What kind of distractions do you anticipate? How might you resolve them?

3. What do you consider to be your most urgent spiritual needs at the moment? What sins do you struggle with the most? It may be helpful to write these in a prayer journal so that you can better note your progress three, six, or twelve months down the road.

## Scripture for Meditation

The first step toward Wisdom is an earnest desire for discipline. (Wisd. 6:17)

## Meditation 1: Creation

*Preparation*

1. Place yourself in the presence of God.
2. Ask the Holy Spirit to inspire your prayer.

*Considerations*

1. Consider the great age of the universe and all the time that passed before you existed.
2. Consider that God created you intentionally at a particular time and place. He did this without your help, purely because He is good.
3. God could have created you as anything, but He made you human, possessing the highest nature in the visible world, made in His very own image (Gen. 1:27), capable of eternal life and union with Him.

*Affections and Resolutions*

1. Humble yourself before God. Pray: "My life is nothing before you. Every man is but a breath" (Ps. 39:6).
2. Thank God for your existence. Pray: "My great and good Creator, how great is my debt to you since you were moved to draw me out of nothing and by your mercy make me what I am! What can I ever

do to bless your holy name in a worthy manner and to render thanks to your immense mercy?"[31]

3. Rebuke yourself for all the times you have failed to love God as He deserves by straying from His goodness and embracing sin.

4. Resolve to change your life and to follow God; to embrace the life God has given you and to live it in obedience to His will.

*Conclusion*

1. Give thanks to God.

2. Pray: "O my God, with all my heart I offer you the being you have given me. I dedicate and consecrate it to you. Strengthen me in these affections and resolutions."

3. Pray: *Our Father ... Hail Mary ... Glory be ...*

4. Reflect on your time of prayer and make a spiritual nosegay to carry with you throughout the day.

---

[31] Ryan translation.

## Meditation 2: Purpose

*Preparation*

1. Place yourself in the presence of God.
2. Ask the Holy Spirit to inspire your prayer.

*Considerations*

1. God does not need you, but He loves you. God is perfect and needs nothing outside of Himself. Yet in His goodness, He has made you to be in relationship with Him. For this purpose, He has given you a mind to know Him and a will to love Him. He has given you senses to know the world He has made, so that you may know the glory of His works. He has given you a tongue to speak His praise. All of your faculties were made for Him.
2. As your purpose is to know, love and serve God, any action contrary to this purpose should be rejected as foolish vanity.
3. Consider the emptiness of a life without this divine and eternal purpose.

*Affections and Resolutions*

1. Humble yourself. Rebuke your soul for all the times it did not consider its purpose. Pray: "What did I think about, O my God, when I did not think

of you? What did I remember when I forgot you? What did I love when I did not love you?"[32]

2. Renounce vain thoughts, useless ambition, wasted deeds, self-indulgence, and any activity that does not bring you closer to God.

3. Turn to God. Pray: "My God and my Savior, you shall be the sole object of my thoughts. Every day of my life I will remember your mercy and your goodness. You are the joy of my heart."

*Conclusion*

1. Give thanks to God.

2. Pray: "Lord, grant me grace that I might attain my purpose of eternal union with you, through the merits of the Blood shed by your Son upon the Cross for me."

3. Pray: *Our Father ... Hail Mary ... Glory be ...*

4. Reflect on your time of prayer and make a spiritual nosegay to carry with you throughout the day.

[32]   Ryan translation.

## MEDITATION 3: BLESSINGS

*Preparation*
1. Place yourself in the presence of God.
2. Ask the Holy Spirit to inspire your prayer.

*Considerations*
1. Consider the many material blessings you have received from God: your body and the means to sustain it, including food, air, water, clothing, and shelter. Consider all that God has given you above and beyond these basic needs: family, friends, and comforts. Think of all those who go without many of these blessings.
2. Consider the many spiritual blessings you have received from God. He has adopted you as His own child in Baptism by incorporating you into the Body of His Son. He has given you teachers and pastors so that you might know of Him. Recall how often He has forgiven your sins and how patient He has been with your repentance. Think of how He has nourished you with His own Body and Blood in the Eucharist.

*Affections and Resolutions*
1. Marvel at God's boundless generosity.
2. Rebuke yourself for past ingratitude.

3. Resolve no longer to be disloyal or ungrateful to your great Benefactor.
4. Resolve to make use of the means provided by the Church to help you love God, especially prayer and the sacraments.

*Conclusion*

1. Give thanks to God for His many blessings and the knowledge He has given you of His blessings.
2. Pray: "What am I, Lord, that you are mindful of me? Yet you have made me little less than a god, and crowned me with glory and honor" (see Ps. 8:5-6).
3. Pray: *Our Father … Hail Mary … Glory be …*
4. Reflect on your time of prayer and make a spiritual nosegay to carry with you throughout the day.

## Meditation 4: Sin

*Preparation*

1. Place yourself in the presence of God.
2. Ask the Holy Spirit to inspire your prayer.

*Considerations*

1. Think back to the first time you did something you knew was wrong. How young were you then? Think of all the sins you have committed since then, in act or in thought, against God, against neighbor, and against yourself. Consider the evil you have done and the good you have failed to do.
2. Consider that the sins you can remember are only a drop in the ocean of sins you have committed over the course of your life.
3. Consider how you have misused the blessings God has given you and how your sins have prevented the grace of the sacraments from bearing the fruit God desires them to bear in your life. How many times have you ignored or resisted the Spirit's calls to repentance?

*Affections and Resolutions*

1. Admonish yourself. Pray: "Lord, I am not worthy to come before you. Not one of the faculties you have given me to serve you has been left uncorrupted

by my sin. I have not loved you, my neighbor, or myself as I ought. Like the Prodigal Son, I no longer deserve to be called your child" (see Luke 15:18–19).

2. Ask God for forgiveness. Pray, "O God, be merciful to me, a sinner (Luke 18:13). Heal me, although I have sinned against you (Ps. 41:5)."

3. Resolve, with the help of God's grace, never again to abandon yourself to sin, to root out the disordered desires of your heart that lead to sin, and to do penance as a sign of your sorrow for your sin and your love for God.

*Conclusion*

1. Give thanks to God for His mercy.

2. Offer Him your heart. Ask Him to cleanse it of all evil desires.

3. Pray: *Our Father … Hail Mary … Glory be …*

4. Reflect on your time of prayer and make a spiritual nosegay to carry with you throughout the day.

## Meditation 5: Death

*Preparation*
1. Place yourself in the presence of God.
2. Ask the Holy Spirit to inspire your prayer.

*Considerations*
1. Imagine your death. Consider that you do not know its hour. It may happen today, tomorrow, or many years from now. But it will happen. Will it be in the winter or in the summer? Will you be awake or asleep? Will it happen suddenly? Will you have time to prepare? Will a priest be present to anoint you and hear your final confession? You cannot know the answer to any of these questions.
2. Consider the ways you have passed your time in this life, all your occupations and amusements. What significance do they have at your final hour? How important will your acts of love seem to you then? How unimportant your acts of selfishness?
3. Imagine your soul saying goodbye to all the things of this world; your possessions, your friends and family members, and finally to your own body, which will be laid in the grave to decompose. Who on earth will remember you a year after you have died? Ten years after? A century after? A thousand years after?

4. After leaving your body, your soul will proceed along one of two paths. It will go to join the Lord in Heaven or will go to be eternally apart from Him in Hell. Which path will it take? It can only be the path it began in this life.

*Affections and Resolutions*

1. Detach yourself from the things of this world: not because they are evil but because they are temporary and you must one day leave them.
2. As you do not know the hour that God will call you from this world, resolve to be ready to leave it at any time by remaining in God's grace.

*Conclusion*

1. Pray to God that He may spare you from an unprepared death.
2. Pray: *Our Father ... Hail Mary ... Glory be ...*
3. Reflect on your time of prayer and make a spiritual nosegay to carry with you throughout the day.

## MEDITATION 6: JUDGMENT

*Preparation*

1. Place yourself in the presence of God.
2. Ask the Holy Spirit to inspire your prayer.

*Considerations*

1. Consider that just as you will die one day, so will this world. The final chapter in the story will be written. Time will come to an end.

2. All of humanity will rise from the dead. Some will be beautiful; others ugly and vile. All will stand (you among them) before God and His angels. Before Him will be the Cross, shining brighter than the sun; a sign of mercy for the good and of judgment for the wicked.

3. The sins of all will be revealed, as will the repentance of the good and the irrepentance of the evil. The good will glorify God's mercy, and the evil will glorify God's justice, but all will glorify God. Christ will separate these two groups, who will never be together again.

4. To one group He will say, "Depart from me, you accursed, into the eternal fire prepared for the devil and his angels" (Matt. 25:41). Consider the weight of the final words these prideful souls will

hear from Jesus. *Depart.* That single word is the ultimate curse of an eternity without God.

5. To the other He will say, "Come, you who are blessed by my Father. Inherit the kingdom prepared for you from the foundation of the world" (Matt. 25:34). Consider the sweetness of these words. *Come.* With this word, God draws the blessed to Himself, to share in His life for all eternity. All blessings are contained within this one word of blessing.

*Affections and Resolutions*

1. Reject your sins, for they are the only thing that can condemn you.
2. Embrace God's mercy, for it is the only thing that can save you.
3. Examine your conscience. Resolve to make a good confession.

*Conclusion*

1. Thank God for giving you the means of salvation through Christ.
2. Offer Him your heart and ask for the grace of true repentance.
3. Pray: *Our Father ... Hail Mary ... Glory be ...*
4. Reflect on your time of prayer and make a spiritual nosegay to carry with you throughout the day.

## Meditation 7: Hell

*Preparation*

1. Place yourself in the presence of God.
2. Ask the Holy Spirit to inspire your prayer.

*Considerations*

1. What do you imagine Hell is like? Jesus compared Hell to Gehenna, a valley near Jerusalem where Canaanites once practiced child sacrifice and where, in Jesus' time, the bodies of criminals and unclean animals and garbage were burned. It was a place to dispose of unwanted things that had no purpose.

2. St. Francis de Sales describes Hell as a place where our senses will be punished according to the sins we committed with them. "The eyes, as the result of their false and evil gazing, will endure the horrible sight of devils.... The ears, which delighted in unholy conversation, will never hear aught but weeping, lamentations and despair, and so with the other senses."

3. The primary punishment of Hell is eternal separation from God. This helps us to understand how Hell is not only compatible with God's love but is demanded by it. God made us to love Him, and love must be freely given, or it is not love at all. To love God, it must also be possible for us to reject

God. Consider the gravity of this terrifying possibility (see CCC 1033).

*Affections and Resolutions*

1. Confess that you have many times lived your life without any consideration of God and therefore deserved Hell.
2. Resolve to follow the opposite path now. Knowing your freely chosen sin to be the one thing that can separate you from God, resolve to avoid even the near occasion of sin (those things that you know lead you into sin, even though they may not themselves be sinful).

*Conclusion*

1. Give thanks to God for saving you from the fires of Hell.
2. Pray: *Our Father ... Hail Mary ... Glory be ...*
3. Reflect on your time of prayer and make a spiritual nosegay to carry with you throughout the day.

MEDITATION 8: HEAVEN

*Preparation*

1. Place yourself in the presence of God.
2. Ask the Holy Spirit to inspire your prayer.

*Considerations*

1. How do you imagine Heaven? St. Paul says, "No eye has seen, nor ear heard, nor the heart of man conceived, what God has prepared for those who love him" (1 Cor. 2:9, RSVCE).

2. Imagine the beauty of a star-filled sky on a clear night. Now imagine the beauty of a perfect day with the sun bright and warm overhead. Now combine the beauty of this perfect day and perfect night, so that the light of the sun does not in any way diminish the light of the stars. St. Francis says, "assuredly all this beauty falls immeasurably short of Paradise."

3. Consider the citizens of Heaven; the angels in their choirs, the apostles, the martyrs, and all the saints. The least of them is more beautiful than anything on this earth. How beautiful are they all together, living in perfect harmony with one another and with God, "sharing the delights of a friendship which can never know any interruptions." St. Francis describes them as "happy birds,

hovering and singing forever in the atmosphere of Divinity," eternally blessed by their Father.

*Affections and Resolutions*

1. Marvel at this heavenly country. Reproach yourself for ever jeopardizing your heavenly citizenship. How could you forsake such infinite and eternal delights for such trivial and unsatisfying pleasures?
2. Pray: "O my good and gracious Lord, since it has pleased you to lead me back onto your paths, never more will I depart from them. Forward then, O my soul! Let us hasten onwards to this everlasting rest, let us press forward to this blessed Land of Promise."
3. Resolve to forsake all things that could hinder you on this journey.

*Conclusion*

1. Pray: "O my Jesus, lead all souls to Heaven, especially those most in need of Thy mercy."
2. Pray: *Our Father ... Hail Mary ... Glory be ...*
3. Reflect on your time of prayer and make a spiritual nosegay to carry with you throughout the day.

## Meditation 9: Your Choice

*Preparation*

1. Place yourself in the presence of God.
2. Ask the Holy Spirit to inspire your prayer.

*Considerations*

1. Imagine yourself on a wide, open plain, alone with your guardian angel. He opens the veil of this word to you, revealing Heaven above, with all its delights, and Hell below, with all its torments.

2. Consider that this is not an imaginary scenario. You are truly placed, at this very moment, between Heaven and Hell. Both are possibilities. You must make a choice, and the choice you make in this life will be eternal in the next.

3. Consider that although God gives you complete freedom in making this choice, He desires above all that you choose to be with Him in Heaven and promises every necessary grace to bring you there. Your guardian angel urges you to choose Heaven and offers you a thousand means of help. You see Jesus looking down from Heaven with love. You hear Him calling you: "Come, O my beloved!" You see His Blessed Mother with Him. She tells you to be brave. She is praying for you. You see the countless saints, eager for you to join their blessed

company. They tell you that the path to Heaven is not as difficult as the world would have you believe; indeed, they found it to be sweet.

*Affections and Resolutions*

1. Renounce Hell now and forever, not because you fear its torments but because you cannot tolerate the loss of God.
2. Make a conscious choice to have Heaven as your eternal home. Accept God's mercy and the love of Christ. Thank God for preparing a place for you in Paradise.
3. Accept the help of the Blessed Virgin, your guardian angel, and all the saints. They are your sure companions on this heavenly journey.

*Conclusion*

1. Give thanks to God.
2. Pray: *Our Father ... Hail Mary ... Glory be ...*
3. Reflect on your time of prayer and make a spiritual nosegay to carry with you throughout the day.

## Meditation 10: Devotion

*Preparation*

1. Place yourself in the presence of God.
2. Ask the Holy Spirit to inspire your prayer.

*Considerations*

1. Imagine yourself once more on an open plain with your guardian angel. To the left you see Satan seated on a throne as ruler of this world. He is surrounded by a swarm of people who hail him as lord. You see their faces. Some are contorted with hatred and anger. Others are weary, weighed down by worry as they seek fortune or fame. Some are twisted with lust and envy. They are busy with empty and unsatisfying pursuits. None are at rest. None know peace. There is no love between them.
2. To your right is Jesus crucified. He is praying for those tormented souls to be free. Around Him is a great throng of men and women, old and young, each with his or her guardian angel, serving Jesus and loving one another. They live in peace, honoring Christ by their mutual affection. Some suffer affliction but are not discouraged. Their Savior comforts them. All hold Christ in the center of their hearts. Jesus calls to you from the cross: "Come, my beloved. Share my crown."

3. You have rejected Hell but have not yet entered Heaven. You still stand between the two in this life. "Salvation is not a matter of words uttered today, but of action which continues to the end by the power of faith.... Do not be anointed with the foul stench of the prince of this world ... or he will enslave you and rob you of the life which is set before you."[33]

*Affections and Resolutions*

1. Renounce Satan and all his empty promises.
2. Enthrone Christ in your heart. Resolve to live a life of devotion with the Virgin Mary as your guide and your guardian angel as your aid.

*Conclusion*

1. Give thanks to God.
2. Pray: *Our Father ... Hail Mary ... Glory be ...*
3. Reflect on your time of prayer and make a spiritual nosegay to carry with you throughout the day.

---

[33] St. Ignatius of Antioch, *Letter to the Ephesians.*

# 7

# Making a General Confession

Having made the previous meditations, you will now be ready to make your general confession. Before doing so, some practical preparation is in order. You should make an appointment with your confessor and let him know what type of confession this will be. A devotional confession of this kind will take more time than a typical confession, so you shouldn't just hop in line during the regular Confession time at your parish. Making an appointment will help keep you and your confessor from feeling rushed.

The idea of a general confession is to confess all the sins of your life, not just those committed since your last Confession. One point must be made clear: this is not to call into question the validity of any past confession. You are confessing anew even sins already forgiven as an act of devotion and not due to any doubt about the efficacy of God's mercy in the sacrament.

> The confession (or disclosure) of sins, even from a simply human point of view, frees us and facilitates our reconciliation with others. Through such an admission man looks squarely at the sins he is guilty of, takes responsibility for them, and thereby opens himself again to God and to the communion of the Church in order to make a new future possible (CCC 1455).

It is this renewed openness to God that you are seeking. Taking ownership once more of past sins is not only humbling; it also reminds us of God's love and limitless forgiveness. *I did all that, and God still loves me! How amazing is that?*

Before your general confession, you should make an extended examination of conscience over the course of several days. Prayerfully read through the Ten Commandments (Exod. 20:1–17), meditating on all the ways you have failed to live by them. Prayerfully read through the Beatitudes (Matt. 5:3–12), meditating on how you have fallen short of the standard of holiness they set. Read over the section in the *Catechism* on the virtues (CCC 1803–1829) and reflect on how they are lacking in your life. There are many guides available to use for an examination of conscience. If you do not have one, your pastor or spiritual director can provide you with one.[34]

In an ordinary confession, we are usually advised to confess our sins in *number and kind*; for example, "I took the Lord's name in vain six times" or "I lied to my spouse twice." A general confession will be different by necessity. When confessing the sins we have committed since our last confession (assuming we go regularly), we can usually recall them specifically. Confessing a lifetime of sins is another matter!

Some of the sins you confess will necessarily be general. If there were years of your life when you were addicted to pornography, or habitually took the Lord's name in vain, it will be impossible for you to recall each specific instance. You will need to speak of these sins in general terms: "I was addicted to pornography for ten years" or "When I was a teenager, my relationship with my mother was not good. I frequently violated the fourth commandment by not honoring her, and I lied to her on multiple occasions."

---

[34] The meditations provided in part 5 of this book may also serve as an extended examination of conscience.

But as you prayerfully reflect back on your past life, certain sins will stand out as particularly significant; perhaps due to their gravity, their unresolved nature, or because some aspect of forgiveness is yet lacking. Make special note of these. There is a reason God is bringing these particular sins to your mind. You may even find yourself recalling things you haven't thought of in years.

You should make a list of these sins as they occur to you. You might recoil at the idea of writing down your sins—what if someone finds the list! But this can be done in a shorthand way that preserves the seal of the confessional. Start a page in the back of your prayer journal, and as sins come to mind during prayer, write down a word or phrase that will be meaningful to you but meaningless to anyone else. For example, if you bullied a boy named Michael Smith in the seventh grade, jot down the initials "M. S." You will know exactly what that means, but the details of your sin will remain private. Making a list beforehand and having it with you in the confessional will ease your anxiety about forgetting any sin you wanted to confess.

When it is time for your general confession, you should enter the confessional with humility and confidence. St. Francis de Sales says, "If we are truly humble, we shall grieve bitterly over our sin because it offends God, but we shall find sweetness in accusing ourselves, because in so doing we honor Him; and we shall find relief in fully revealing our complaints to our physician." There is something very freeing about being completely open about the worst parts of ourselves; not hiding our faults and failings, not wearing any mask, but being completely open to the gaze of One who loves us. It is something found in only the most intimate friendships.

St. Francis advises you to "speak simply" as you confess your sins, imagining yourself kneeling at the foot of the Cross and

Christ's Precious Blood pouring down upon you to wash you clean. Even though it is not His physical blood being poured on you, the grace won by the shedding of His blood is being poured out on you as you confess. Every time a sin is removed from your heart as you speak it aloud, Christ's mercy comes flooding in to fill the space that sin once inhabited.

After confessing all your sins, listen attentively to the direction of the priest. He is the Lord's minister, to whom Jesus said, "Whoever listens to you, listens to me" (Luke 10:16). Say in your heart, "Speak, LORD, for your servant is listening" (1 Sam. 3:9). Ask any clarifying questions you need to. Resolve to follow your confessor's advice, and then, when prompted by your confessor, make an Act of Contrition. You may wish to use the following, which has been adapted from St. Francis's "Resolution to Serve God" (part I, chapter 20). If you do make use of this prayer in the confessional, make sure your confessor is aware that you will be making a longer than usual Act of Contrition. Otherwise, you may pray this prayer privately at the conclusion of your general confession.

## ACT OF CONTRITION

O God, I come before you, and all your angels and saints, as your unworthy servant whom you have created out of nothing and upon whom you have bestowed so many unearned blessings, and to whom you have shown such infinite patience. I fully acknowledge that I have offended you by my sins, which I have committed through my own weakness, pride, and ingratitude. Because of my transgressions against your goodness and love, I deserve damnation and I am guilty of the death and passion of your Son, who died for my sins upon the Cross. I acknowledge and embrace that same Cross as the sure and only hope of my salvation.

I renew in your presence today the promises of my baptism. I renounce Satan, all his works, and all his empty promises. I renounce sin and all affection to sin, so as to live in freedom as a child of God. Turning away forever from the father of lies and prince of this world, I turn toward you, the Father of Truth and King of Heaven, and throw myself upon your mercy. I renounce the devil, the world, and the flesh and irrevocably resolve to love and serve you now and forever. I consecrate to you my mind, my heart, my body and my soul and all their faculties. I will never again use any part of my being in a way contrary to your gracious will and purpose.

If ever I should fall once more into sin, through temptation by the devil or by my own human weakness, I resolve with the help of your Holy Spirit to rise again as soon as I perceive my fall and seek refuge in your mercy without any hesitation or delay.

I make this resolution today in the presence of your Son Jesus Christ, Mary his Immaculate Mother, Joseph her most chaste spouse, and all the saints. May you receive my contrition and resolution as a most fragrant offering. As you have been pleased to inspire within me the desire to serve you, grant me also the strength and the grace needed to do so faithfully and well.

O my God, you are my God, the God of my heart, the God of my soul, the God of my spirit; I acknowledge you as such and adore you now and for all eternity. Amen.

Now listen attentively to the words of absolution spoken by your confessor. These are the words spoken to you by Jesus from His throne of mercy. "Through the ministry of the Church, may God give you pardon and peace, and I absolve you from your sins, in the name of the Father, and of the Son, and of the Holy Spirit."[35]

Having been reconciled to God and His Church through the sacramental grace of our confession, we can now devote ourselves to the great work of ongoing conversion. The *Catechism* teaches, "Interior repentance is a radical reorientation of our whole life, a return, a conversion to God with all our heart, an end of sin, a turning away from evil, with repugnance toward the evil actions we have committed. At the same time it entails the desire and resolution to change one's life, with hope in God's mercy and trust in the help of his grace" (1431).

Conversion is the work of a lifetime. St. Francis de Sales says, "Your soul will be purged from sin and from all affection for sin," but he admits that "such affections easily spring up again in the soul because of our infirmity and concupiscence, which may be mortified but will never die as long as we live here upon earth."[36]

---

[35] *Ordo Paenitentiae* 46.
[36] Ryan translation.

*Questions for Reflection*

1. If you have made a general or devotional confession before, what were some of the spiritual benefits you experienced?
2. If you have never made a devotional confession, were any of your confessions more meaningful than others? What contributed to their impact?
3. Spend time in preparation by finding different examinations of conscience you can pray with and making an appointment with your confessor.

*Scripture for Meditation*

The scribes and the Pharisees brought a woman who had been caught in adultery and made her stand in the middle. They said to him, "Teacher, this woman was caught in the very act of committing adultery. Now in the law, Moses commanded us to stone such women. So what do you say?" They said this to test him, so that they could have some charge to bring against him.

Jesus bent down and began to write on the ground with his finger. But when they continued asking him, he straightened up and said to them, "Let the one among you who is without sin be the first to throw a stone at her." Again he bent down and wrote on the ground. And in response, they went away one by one, beginning with the elders. So he was left alone with the woman before him.

Then Jesus straightened up and said to her, "Woman, where are they? Has no one condemend you?" She replied, "No one, sir." Then Jesus said, "Neither do I condemn you. Go, and from now on do not sin any more." (John 8:3–11)

# 8

# Ongoing Conversion and Purification

I was baptized when I was twenty-three years old. I recall looking forward to that day with great anticipation. I was going to be born again as a child of God! I was going to be cleansed of all my sins, and the Holy Spirit was going to dwell within me, strengthening me with His gifts. What would that be like, I wondered, to be free of sin? I was not naive enough to think I would be completely free of temptation, but I imagined it would somehow be lessened.

That was not my experience, as I confessed to my pastor sometime later. "If anything," I said, "I feel more tempted. It's like I'm hyperaware of all the opportunities around me to sin every day." My wise pastor assured me that that was normal. "Of course you are more aware of sin," he told me. "You notice dirt more when you are clean."

St. Francis de Sales observes that bright light allows us to see more clearly all our warts and wrinkles in the mirror. "Even so, as the Holy Spirit enlightens our conscience we perceive more clearly and distinctly the sins, inclinations, and imperfections which hinder us in attaining to true devotion." The same light that shows us our imperfections also kindles in us the desire to be free of them.

Sin is an imperfection. One of the Hebrew words we translate as "sin" is *cheit*, which means "to miss the mark." It's an archery term. But we can miss the mark by different degrees. If I am aiming for the bull's-eye and my arrow lands a couple of inches to the right, I've missed the mark but still landed on the target. But if I fire my arrow in the direction opposite the target, I've missed the target entirely and probably shot something I shouldn't have been aiming for! I've missed the mark in both cases, but the former is an imperfection (there's always room for improvement), while the latter is radical negligence (they ought to kick me off the target range for safety violations).

St. John says, "All wrongdoing is sin, but there is sin that is not deadly" (1 John 5:17). So the Church distinguishes between mortal and venial sin. Mortal sin is deadly to the life of grace because it is incompatible with charity. Venial sin only weakens charity. It's not deadly, but it is contrary to devotion. (For a treatment of mortal and venial sin, see CCC 1854–1864.)

Just because venial sin is not deadly to the life of grace doesn't mean it shouldn't be taken seriously. St. Francis de Sales warns that after our conversion, we will still discover within ourselves an inclination to venial sins. The practice of devotion is meant to help us root out this inclination before it festers into something worse.

"We can never be wholly free from venial sins," St. Francis writes, "at least not for any length of time, but we can be without affection for them. There is a wide difference between a chance falsehood concerning some trivial matter, which is the result of carelessness, and taking pleasure in falsehood or deliberately tell-ing lies."[37]

He warns against "willingly harboring venial sins in our con-science," by telling ourselves that they aren't so bad. "Venial sins do not destroy the soul, but they hinder devotion, and so clog the powers of the soul with bad habits and inclinations that it loses that active charity which is the lifespring of devotion."

---

[37] Quotations in this chapter are taken from part 1, chapter 22.

He uses the image of a beehive clogged with spider webs. The spiders do not kill the bees, but their webs spoil the honey.

Some slight falsehood, some lack of self-control in word or action, in dress, in occupation, in amusement—these will leave no lasting evil if, like spider's webs, they are banished from our conscience as soon as perceived, just as the bees drive out the intruding spider. But if we permit them to remain, still more if we take any pleasure in them and suffer them to multiply, soon our honey will be lost, and the hive of our conscience will be soiled and damaged.

In addition to the moral imperfection of venial sin, we each have natural imperfections. We may naturally tend to sadness, anger, impatience, grumpiness, weariness, rashness, and so forth. These are not sins but can make us more easily disposed to certain sins. We therefore must work to correct these natural flaws in our character. St. Francis says, "There is no disposition so good by nature that it cannot acquire bad habits, neither is there any disposition naturally so perverse that by the grace of God, united to diligence and industry, it may not be conquered and subdued."

By rooting out affection for venial sin and seeking to overcome even natural imperfections, we secure ourselves against offending God by falling into mortal sin. In the next section, St. Francis de Sales offers ways for us to do just that.

## Questions for Reflection

1.  How can tolerance or acceptance of even venial sins lead to more serious sins?
2.  Why is it important always to aim for perfection, even if we know we will fall short of the mark?
3.  How do your natural imperfections make you prone to venial sin (missing the mark)? How can you attempt to correct those flaws?

## Scripture for Meditation

Beloved, we are God's children now; what we shall be has not yet been revealed. We do know that when it is revealed we shall be like him, for we shall see him as he is. Everyone who has this hope based on him makes himself pure, as he is pure. No one who is begotten by God commits sin, because God's seed remains in him; he cannot sin because he is begotten by God. In this way, the children of God and the children of the devil are made plain; no one who fails to act in righteousness belongs to God, nor anyone who does not love his brother. (1 John 3:2–3, 9–10)

Part II

# Planting the Seed

# 1

# Learning to Pray

"How do I pray?" It's not an unreasonable question. We see people sitting or kneeling at prayer, heads bowed and hands folded. But what are they *doing*? Jesus' disciples, after observing Him in prayer, approached Him and said, "Lord, teach us to pray" (Luke 11:1). Show us how to do what You do!

In *An Introduction to the Devout Life*, St. Francis de Sales describes a method of mental prayer that he recommends to his directees. You'll be familiar with the format from the meditations provided in part 1 of this book.

- Place yourself in the presence of God.
- Meditate upon a mystery of the Faith.
- Cultivate affections and make resolutions.
- Conclude in a spirit of grateful humility.
- Finally, make a "spiritual nosegay" to carry your prayer with you throughout the day.

We will describe this method of prayer in more detail in the next few chapters. But before we focus on the *how* of prayer, we need to understand the *why*.

Just as oxygen is necessary for our physical life, so prayer is necessary for our spiritual life. It is like the air we breathe, and this is why St. Paul instructs us to "pray without ceasing" (1 Thess. 5:17). Otherwise, our souls will suffocate. Prayer is therefore not one activity among many for Christians. It is a mode of being, an attitude, and an orientation that we bring to all our endeavors.

Above all, prayer is a relationship. We were made by God for relationship with Him, and as the *Catechism* so succinctly puts it, "that relationship is prayer" (2558).

So the first thing to understand is that Christian prayer, unlike forms of meditation practiced by other religions, is not about learning a method. As Catholic philosopher Peter Kreeft puts it, "The most important thing about prayer is not *how* we do it but *that* we do it. The single most important answer to the question 'How to pray?' is: 'Begin!' "[38]

Like any other skill, prayer takes practice. One doesn't become an expert musician by studying music theory without ever picking up an instrument. Master musicians know the theory, but they have also put in countless hours of practice. The same is true of prayer. We learn by doing.

But prayer is also a relationship. You don't build a relationship with someone by stalking them from a distance. You must take that first awkward step of beginning a conversation with someone you don't know very well yet. You become friends with someone by spending time with that person. Prayer is time spent with God.

There are many ways to pray, but St. Francis de Sales especially recommends daily mental prayer. Unlike vocal prayer, which is spoken aloud—and which the *Catechism* also calls "an essential element of Christian life" (2701)—mental prayer consists of silent meditation on the mysteries of God. Just as children learn to speak gradually by imitating their parents, "if you habitually meditate upon [God]," St. Francis writes, "your whole soul will be filled with him, you will learn his expression, and learn to frame your actions after his example."[39]

---

[38] Peter J. Kreeft, *Catholic Christianity* (San Francisco: Ignatius Press, 2001), 376.

[39] Quotations in this chapter are taken from part 2, chapter 1.

St. Francis recommends spending an hour each day in mental prayer. An hour may seem daunting to someone just starting out, but do not be dissuaded. As prayer is less about technique than it is about fostering a relationship, we shouldn't be overly scrupulous about praying for a specific length of time.

How long does a conversation with a friend last? As long as it needs to. You talk until the conversation comes to a natural conclusion, and if a pressing matter pulls you away before it is over, you try to resume it at your next opportunity. It should be the same with prayer. We should pray until our prayer is concluded, regardless of how long it takes. But St. Francis's recommendation of an hour is helpful because it gives us an idea of a practical norm. It is something to aim for, even if we have to build up to it.

If you don't think you have an hour to spare, consider that God gives everyone the same twenty-four hours in a day. It is up to us to use them wisely. Don't think of prayer as something to be done in your "spare time." Offer God your firstfruits, not the leftover parts of your day! Interestingly, St. Francis also advises against spending *more* than an hour in prayer, lest we be tempted to mistake length for quality.

We pray in both body and spirit; therefore, much of St. Francis's advice is practical. He recommends that we pray in the morning "because then your mind is less cumbered and more vigorous after the night's rest" and "not directly after a meal," as that might tend to make us sleepy. He also recommends praying in a church, if possible, because it is not always easy to "ensure an uninterrupted hour at home."

Our homes tend to be full of distractions. If we live with others, our homes are not always guaranteed places of quiet. Even if we live alone, home is still the place where we *live*. By this, I mean it is where we cook meals, wash dishes, fold laundry, watch movies, read books, take naps, vacuum floors, and practice our hobbies.

When we pray at home, we are surrounded by a hundred other things we could be doing. This can make focusing on prayer difficult, especially if we have not yet developed a strong discipline of prayer. Churches have the benefit of being places designed to help us focus our minds and hearts on God.

On the other hand, home will often be the most convenient place to pray. We should never neglect our duty to pray because we cannot get to church. As the Carmelite monk Br. Lawrence wrote to one of his spiritual directees:

> It is not necessary for being with God to be always at church. We may make an oratory of our heart wherein to retire from time to time to converse with him in meekness, humility, and love. Everyone is capable of such familiar conversation with God, some more, some less. Let us begin, then.[40]

When praying at home, it helps to have a dedicated place for prayer, even if it is only a chair or a corner in a room. It should be free of clutter and distractions, preferably with a crucifix or an icon of Our Lord nearby to serve as a focal point.

As for the content of prayer, St. Francis de Sales recommends the basics: the Lord's Prayer, the Hail Mary, and the Creed. We may tend to take these simple prayers for granted, but they provide an essential foundation and model for our prayer. It is important that our individual prayer be rooted in the traditional prayers of the Church, lest we think our own words to be more worthy than the words Our Lord Himself gave us. This is why St. John Henry Newman advised against seeking novelty in prayer. "Let us be satisfied with sober words which have been ever in use; it will be a great thing if we enter into *them*."[41]

---

[40] *Practice of the Presence of God*, seventh letter.
[41] Newman, *Sermon 11*

## Questions for Reflection

1.  Is there a place in your home suitable for daily prayer?
    If not, what are some practical ways you might create
    one? How might you find time in your schedule to visit
    a church a few times each week for prayer?

2.  As prayer is a relationship, what expectations do you
    have for God in this relationship? How do you antici-
    pate that He might communicate with you? In what
    ways can you be attentive to how He answers your prayer
    throughout the day?

3.  Are there traditional prayers of the Church that you es-
    pecially love? Do you sometimes take traditional prayers
    for granted because they are familiar? What might you
    do to gain a "fresh perspective" and rediscover the value
    of these traditional prayers?

## Scripture for Meditation

[Jesus] was praying in a certain place, and when he had
finished, one of his disciples said to him, "Lord, teach us
to pray just as John taught his disciples." He said to them,
"When you pray, say: Father, hallowed be your name, your
kingdom come. Give us each day our daily bread and forgive us our sins for we ourselves forgive everyone in debt to
us, and do not subject us to the final test." (Luke 11:1-4)

## 2

# Preparing to Pray

Prayer is spiritual exercise. Just as your body responds better to physical exercise if you stretch and warm up first, prayer also requires a bit of a "warm-up" for us to gain the most benefit from it. St. Francis de Sales says we should always begin our prayer by placing ourselves in the presence of God and invoking His help. We discussed the need to place ourselves in the presence of God in chapter 6 of part 1. Here, St. Francis offers suggestions to help us put this into practice.

We begin with "a keen and attentive realizing of God's omnipresence." God is everywhere. We are always in His presence, whether we realize it or not. Just as birds fly through the air and fish swim in the water, "in him we live and move and have our being" (Acts 17:28). But just as birds and fish are largely unaware of the air and water even though it surrounds them, we are often unaware of God. St. Francis says, "We all know [God is omnipresent] as an intellectual truth, but we do not always receive and act upon it.... For though as a mere matter of reasoning we know that he is everywhere, if we do not think about it, the result is the same as if we did not know it" (2, 2). This is why it is necessary consciously to recall our mind to the truth of God's presence before we pray so that we can be attentive to Him. We should also remember that God is not only present in the world around us; He is also present *in us*, in our hearts and souls. God is not just "out there." He is "in here."

The Incarnation also provides us with a way to visualize God's presence. In Christ, God has a human face. St. Francis says to imagine "the Savior in his humanity as actually present with us; just as we do with the friends we love." If you are in a church praying before the Blessed Sacrament, "this Presence becomes no longer imaginary, but actual" (2, 2).

Recalling our mind to the presence of God is the prerequisite to prayer, not prayer itself, so we should not spend too much time in this effort. In placing yourself in God's presence, St. Francis says, "let what you do be short and simple" (2, 2).

Then, "having placed your soul in the presence of God, you must humble it with deep reverence" (2, 3). We easily forget what a great privilege it is for us mere creatures to come before our God in prayer. It is not something we deserve or have earned but a privilege made possible for us by Christ, who tore open the veil between this world and heaven (Matt. 27:51) and makes us temples of the Holy Spirit (1 Cor. 6:19). St. Francis suggests making a brief, earnest petition as we begin our prayer, such as "Do not drive me from before your face, nor take from me your holy Spirit" (Ps. 51:13) or "Let your face shine upon your servant; teach me your statutes" (Ps. 119:135). Then invoke the intercession of your guardian angel and any saint who may be connected with the object of your meditation. Ask them to add their prayers to yours.

Finally, St. Francis de Sales recommends that we enter into our meditation through what some call the "composition of place" or the "inner lesson." We would call it using our imagination.

> This is simply representing to ourselves by the aid of the
> imagination the mystery on which we would meditate,
> as though it were going on before our eyes. For instance,
> if the subject of your meditation is the crucified Savior,

imagine yourself on Mount Calvary, beholding and hearing all the events of his Passion; and represent to yourself all that the Evangelists describe.... By the help of this vivid imagination we can the better fix our mind upon the proposed subject of meditation, and refrain from wandering thoughts. (2, 4)

This exercise of the imagination is possible when we are meditating upon a visible mystery of our Faith, such as the Crucifixion, the Nativity, or any other event in the life of Christ. However, when we meditate upon an invisible mystery of the Faith, such as "God's greatness, the excellence of goodness, the end of our creation, and such invisible things, we cannot employ this active imagination." St. Francis says, "We can certainly use similitudes and comparisons to assist our reflections; but there is some effort in this, and I would have you act with great simplicity, and not fatigue your mind with labored thoughts."

Though our warm-up to prayer should be brief, we should not neglect to give it proper attention. It helps to focus our minds and hearts on the greatness of our task and helps us, in human terms, to transition from our everyday activities to the sacred work of prayer.

## Questions for Reflection

1. Do you find it challenging to remember that you are in God's presence? What prevents you from being more mindful of this reality?

2. The *Catechism* calls humility "the foundation of prayer" (2559). Why do you think this is? What is the relationship between humility and prayer?

3. How do you feel about using your imagination to aid you in prayer? If you don't have a particularly vivid imagination, what are some ways you can help your mind enter into the subject of your prayer?

## Scripture for Meditation

O God, you are my God—
it is you I seek!
For you my body yearns;
for you my soul thirsts,
In a land parched, lifeless,
and without water.
I look to you in the sanctuary
to see your power and glory.
For your love is better than life;
my lips shall ever praise you! (Ps. 63:1–4)

# 3

# Meditation

You've prepared yourself for prayer by recalling your mind and heart to God's presence. Now what? Here we come to the heart of mental prayer: meditation leading to reflection, affection, and resolution.

When we speak of meditation in the context of Christian prayer, we don't mean the kind of meditation practiced in some Eastern religions, such as transcendental meditation or "mindfulness." Transcendental meditation, from Vedic Hinduism, involves the use of a repeated mantra to allow the mind to "transcend" normal thought. Mindfulness meditation comes from Buddhism and is geared toward helping practitioners be more attentive to the present moment. By contrast, the purpose of Christian meditation is not to center our thoughts or to transcend our thoughts, but to direct our thoughts to God. The *Catechism* calls meditation "a quest" in which "the mind seeks to understand the why and the how of the Christian life" (2705).

Mental prayer involves meditating upon a divine subject. For this, St. Francis especially recommends the Rosary. Its twenty mysteries provide a solid overview of the life of Christ. If you struggle to stay focused on the mysteries as you pray the Rosary, it can be helpful to introduce each decade with a short Scripture reading related to that mystery or to have a visual depiction of the mystery to look at while you pray.

You can also use *lectio divina* (sacred reading) to provide the subject of your meditation. Any Scripture passage will do, but

I especially recommend using the daily Mass readings. There is something very powerful in praying with the same Scripture that the universal Church is praying with around the globe. Spiritual writings from the Church Fathers or other saints, as well as icons and other works of sacred art, can also provide you with subjects for meditation.

Whatever your subject, once you focus on it, you should begin to reflect. What does this mystery *mean*? To me? In my life? The purpose of our reflection is to excite our affections toward God. If we don't find our affections aroused by a particular reflection, St. Francis says not to worry. Just move on gently to another reflection, as a honeybee moves from one flower to another.

It's important to note that St. Francis does not mean *affection* in the common sense of "good feelings toward," although that kind of affection for God is also good. To help us understand what we mean by *affection* in the context of prayer, Cistercian Fr. Eugene Boylan describes it this way in his book, *Difficulties in Mental Prayer*:

> Affections in prayer are essentially acts of the will, by which it moves toward God and elicits other acts of the different virtues, such as faith, hope, love, sorrow, humility, gratitude or praise. In the earlier stages of the spiritual life these affections usually cannot be produced without laborious consideration and tedious effort.... The word *meditation*, in its strict sense, denotes this preparatory work of reflection and consideration. This is not really prayer; it is merely a prelude to prayer. The affections and petitions form the real prayer.[42]

---

[42] Eugene Boylan, *Difficulties in Mental Prayer* (Princeton, NJ: Scepter Publishers, 1943), 17.

Meditation is a means to the end of affection and resolution. In fact, St. Francis tells us that "if the Holy Spirit gives you that warmth of affection and resolution without studied reflection, you have no need of it" (2, 7).

What makes the kind of affection we are talking about different from a feeling? It's not uncommon in prayer to experience certain emotions. Pondering God's love might give you a feeling of happiness and warmth. Reflecting on your sins may give you a feeling of sadness and regret. These are natural feelings and are good. But then again, you may not experience these emotions in prayer. That's also normal. Some people feel emotions more easily or intensely than others. This does not make their prayer more or less worthy.

Affection is a desire that moves your heart toward God. There is a distinction between desire and emotion. Desire has to do with what we want. Emotions come to us (or don't) whether we want them or not. By saying that reflection in prayer should excite affection toward God, St. Francis means that it should increase our desire for God. And that's more a matter of choice than of emotion. We can *choose* to *want* God, whether prayer gives us "warm, fuzzy feelings" or not.

As acts of the will, affections in prayer should lead you to make specific resolutions. How can you put this affection into action? What act of virtue can you make that would express it? Two examples will help illustrate the connection between reflection, affection, and resolution.

Let's say the subject of your meditation is the wonder of creation. You read the first two chapters of Genesis, which describe God's creation of the universe and our place in it. You begin to reflect by asking, *Why should anything exist at all?* You realize that nothing in the universe created itself. Everything is dependent on

God. You reflect that this is also true for you. You did not have to exist. Yet God found it good to bring you into being. This arouses within you certain affections: awe at God's power and generosity, and gratitude for your own existence. What resolutions might you make from these affections? It could be as general as resolving to be more grateful to God for loving you into being. Or it could be something more specific, such as resolving to take better care of your body by quitting smoking or taking better care of your soul by going to Confession more often. The more specific and practical the resolution, the easier it will be to put into practice.

Perhaps another time you are meditating upon the Crucifixion. You compose the scene in your mind by reading the Passion narrative from one of the Gospels or by gazing upon a crucifix. You begin to reflect upon the words of Christ as He is being nailed to the Cross. You find yourself lingering especially on these words: "Father, forgive them, they know not what they do" (Luke 23:34). This stirs in you a desire to forgive those who have harmed you and to love your enemies. That is the affection. You then remember someone who wronged you long ago whom you still hold a grudge against, and you resolve to forgive that person. Or you think of a rude co-worker who frequently makes you angry, and you resolve not to let her inconsiderate words lead you to uncharitable thoughts.

Making practical resolutions from your affections is how these daily meditations will help you grow in devotion and virtue. By making specific resolutions, St. Francis says, "you will correct your faults in a very short time, whereas by [general] affections alone you will do so but slowly and with difficulty" (2, 6).[43]

---

[43] Ross translation.

## Questions for Reflection

1. Besides the Rosary and daily Mass readings, what are some other sources of divine subjects for meditation that you might consider? Are there books or passages from Scripture that you find especially good fodder for prayer?

2. What makes the affections in prayer that St. Francis describes different from simple good feelings toward God or sorrow for your sin that may arise in prayer?

3. Why is it important to form a specific resolution from your affections? How might your progress in devotion be hindered without these resolutions?

## Scripture for Meditation

Blessed is the man who does not walk
in the counsel of the wicked,
Nor stand in the way of sinners,
nor sit in company with scoffers.
Rather, the law of the LORD is his joy;
and on his law he meditates day and night.
He is like a tree
planted near streams of water,
that yields its fruit in due season;
Its leaves never wither;
whatever he does prospers. (Ps. 1:1–3)

# 4

# Concluding Prayer

St. Francis de Sales instructs us to conclude our time of prayer with three simple acts, which he says "should be made with the utmost humility" (2, 7).

*Thanksgiving*: Thank God for giving you good affections and resolutions, and for any special insights you have gained during your meditation.

*Oblation*: Offer to God the merits won by Christ in union with your affections and resolutions.

*Intercession*: Ask God to bless your affections and resolutions and to grant you the grace necessary to fulfill your resolutions. Pray for the Church, your priests, and your family and friends, and ask Our Lady, the angels, and the saints for their intercession.

Finally, St. Francis instructs us to conclude with "the Our Father and Hail Mary, the universal and never-failing petition of the faithful" (2, 7). "One Lord's Prayer said with devotion," St. Francis advises, "is worth more than many recited hastily" (2, 1).

Then don't be too hasty to leave your time of prayer. Spend a few moments making a "spiritual nosegay" as described in chapter 6 of part 1. This will help the fruits of your prayer carry over into your daily life. Think of time spent in dedicated prayer as planting seeds. If the seeds of prayer take root in your heart, they will blossom and bear fruit throughout your life.

St. Francis suggests that, as you conclude your dedicated prayer time, you remain for a brief time in quietness, passing gently from prayer to "needful occupations," retaining as long as possible your holy thoughts and inclinations. "A man who has received a costly vessel full of some precious cordial would carry it most carefully. He would walk slowly, and not look idly about him, but keep his eyes now on the road before him" (2, 7), for fear that a misstep should cause him to spill some of his treasure. We should have a similar attitude after prayer.

St. Francis says:

> You must accustom yourself to go from prayer to whatever occupations may be involved by your station or profession, even though they may seem far distant from the feelings excited in you by that prayer.... Since these duties as well as that of prayer are imposed on us by God, we must pass from one to the other in a devout and humble spirit. (2, 7)

Rather than being distracted from your other duties by times of prayer, your time of dedicated prayer should allow you to perform your other duties more prayerfully. Here we have the great model of the monastery cook Br. Lawrence, who famously said, "The time of business does not with me differ from the time of prayer, and in the noise and clatter of my kitchen, while several persons are at the same time calling for different things, I possess God in as great tranquility as if I were upon my knees at the Blessed Sacrament."[44]

This Carmelite monk recognized that "our sanctification did not depend upon *changing* our works, but in doing that for God's sake which we commonly do for our own ... doing our common business without any view of pleasing men, and (as far as we are

---

[44] *The Practice of the Presence of God*, fourth conversation.

capable) purely for the love of God."[45] Before commencing his daily business, Br. Lawrence would pray:

> *O my God, since Thou art with me, and I must now, in obedience to Thy commands, apply my mind to these outward things, I beseech Thee to grant me the grace to continue in Thy presence; and to this end do Thou prosper me with Thy assistance, receive all my works, and possess all my affections.*[46]

"One way to recollect the mind easily in the time of prayer," the kitchen monk observed, "is not to let it wander too far at other times."[47] In the next chapter, St. Francis de Sales imparts his saintly advice on how to do just that.

Finally, you must remain mindful throughout the day of the resolutions you have made in prayer and actively seek out opportunities to put them into practice. You may find it helpful to make note of these resolutions in a prayer journal, which you can go back and review at regular intervals to note your progress in these virtues. If you discover you have failed to put any resolutions into practice, renew your commitment and ask for God's grace and guidance in helping you to fulfill them. Then look for the opportunities to practice those resolutions that God will provide in answer to that prayer.

---

[45] Ibid.

[46] Ibid.

[47] *The Practice of the Presence of God*, eighth letter.

## Questions for Reflection

1. Do you find it difficult to remain mindful of God during your ordinary daily tasks? What might help you remain more mindful of His presence?
2. Br. Lawrence writes of doing for God what we ordinarily do for man. What difference would that change in attitude make for your daily duties?
3. If you are to look for opportunities to practice your resolutions during the day, how might that impact the kinds of resolutions you make in prayer?

## Scripture for Meditation

Slaves, be obedient to your human masters with fear and trembling, in sincerity of heart, as to Christ, not only when being watched, as currying favor, but as slaves of Christ, doing the will of God from the heart, willingly serving the Lord and not human beings. (Eph. 6:5–7)

# 5

# Praying throughout the Day

In addition to the dedicated time of mental prayer we have been describing, St. Francis de Sales recommends several other ways of praying throughout the day; he calls these "the forerunners and servants of the principal devotion" (2, 10).

He recommends that a brief prayer be made each morning in preparation for the day's tasks. This consists of thanking God for His mercy in preserving you through the night and asking His forgiveness for any sins you might have committed during the previous day. Then recall that the present day is given to you by God to help you prepare for eternity; resolve to use it for that purpose. Run through your day's agenda. Ask God to bless all the activities of your day so that you might do them in His service. What temptations do you anticipate the day might bring? Ask God to preserve you from them. Entrust yourself to God, recognizing that you are incapable of doing good or avoiding evil without His help. Finally, conclude this brief prayer by invoking the intercession of the Blessed Virgin, your guardian angel, and the saints. St. Francis writes that this prayer "should be briefly and heartily performed before you leave your room, so that by this means all you do throughout the day may be refreshed by the blessing of God" (2, 10).

The saint recommends a similar exercise be made in the evening. Before retiring to bed, call to mind the crucified Lord and prostrate yourself before Him in love and humility. Perform a brief examination of conscience by first thanking God for preserving you throughout the day, and then reviewing all you have done that day. Reflect on where you were, whom you were with, and what you did. Were there any ways in which you failed to act in accord with love of God and love of neighbor? "If you have done anything that is good, thank God for it," St. Francis instructs. "If you have sinned in thought, word, or deed, ask his forgiveness, resolving to make confession of the same at the first opportunity, and diligently to amend" (2, 11). End by asking God's protection through the night and invoking the intercession of the Blessed Mother, your angel, and the saints.

By this daily morning prayer, St. Francis says you "open the windows of your soul to the sun of righteousness," and by the evening devotion "you close them against the darkness of Hell" (2, 11).

Besides these brief morning and evening exercises, which can serve as prayerful bookends to your day, St. Francis recommends that you frequently "retire into the solitude of your heart, even whilst you are externally occupied in business or society." Just as birds find rest in their nests and deer seek shade in the forest, your heart "should seek a resting-place on Mount Calvary or in the wounds of our Blessed Lord, or in some other spot close to him." You can make an oratory of your heart in this way even when in the company of others, for as St. Francis points out, "they do but surround your body, not your heart, which should remain alone in the presence of God" (2, 12). I have frequently benefited from such prayerful recollection in conference rooms, in dentist's chairs, in the car, and in the grocery store. No matter where I am, my heart can be on Calvary!

St. Francis also suggests making frequent use of short, spontaneous prayers to keep you mindful of God as you go about the day's business. It can be helpful to have a few short prayers or Scripture verses memorized to be used for this purpose, such as the Jesus Prayer ("Lord Jesus Christ, Son of God, have mercy on me, a sinner," after the publican's prayer in Luke 18:13) or "Blessed be the name of the LORD both now and forever" (Ps. 113:2). St. Francis says even verses from your favorite hymns can serve this purpose, but he writes, "I would advise you not to confine yourself to any formal words; rather use those which are prompted by the feelings of your heart" (2, 13).

Sprinkling these little loving thoughts of God throughout the day should not be difficult. "Such prayer," the saint writes, "may be interwoven with all our business and occupations without hindering them in the slightest degree." It is the most natural thing in the world to think frequently of one you love. As you grow in devotion to God, you will find not only that you think of Him more often and with greater earnestness but that you also begin to see the world through the lens of that love. The whole world reminds you of God. Everything becomes an occasion to praise Him!

St. Francis gives various examples to illustrate this point. I will give one of his and one of my own. St. Francis relates a story about St. Gregory of Nazianzus, who once observed how the waves on the seashore left behind little shells, bits of seaweed, and other small debris. A new wave would come and crash over the shore, dragging some of these things back into the sea and depositing others in its wake. By contrast, he observed how the large rocks on the shore remained immovable as the waves crashed against them. Observing this scene, St. Gregory reflected: The small shells and bits of seaweed were like souls who let themselves be carried away by the pleasures and sorrows of this world. They were at the mercy of the tides of fortune. But the large rocks were like faithful souls standing firm against the world's temptations, even amid the roughest of storms.

# The Devout Life

The next story is from my own experience. I was walking outside in the dark, using a flashlight to guide me. I noticed that the light had two effects. It illuminated the path I was walking on, but it also made everything it was not shining on appear darker, so that I couldn't see anything at all on either side of my path. The light didn't actually make things off the path darker, but because my eyes were adjusted to the light, I couldn't see in the darkness as clearly. This made me think of how Christ is the light of the world (John 8:12). By His light, we see clearly the path we are to follow. As our eyes become adjusted to His light, the things that lie outside that light diminish in the darkness. Christ's light gives us focus, and if we keep our eyes attuned to it, we won't be as easily led astray from the path of righteousness.

St. Francis assures us that it is possible to "extract holy thoughts and pious aspirations from all the various circumstances of our mortal life" (2, 13). Every aspect of creation, every situation that may befall us, can become for us an occasion of prayer if we learn to see it through the holy lens of devotion.

## Questions for Reflection

1.  Are you in the habit of previewing or reviewing your day in the morning and evening? If so, how might you turn this into an occasion of prayer? If not, how could you make this part of your routine?
2.  Which of your daily tasks might you be able to turn into opportunities for prayer?
3.  When has an everyday occurrence reminded you of God or some aspect of God's love? What helped your mind to make that connection?

## Scripture for Meditation

Seven times a day I praise you
because your judgments are righteous.
Lovers of your law have much peace;
for them there is no stumbling block.
I look for your salvation, LORD,
and I fulfill your commandments.
I observe your testimonies;
I love them very much.
I observe your precepts and testimonies;
all my ways are before you. (Ps. 119:164–168)

# 6

# Dryness and Distraction

Dryness in prayer is something even the most devout Christians experience, often for long periods of time, as was the case with St. Teresa of Calcutta. Spiritual dryness is not so much a feeling as it is the absence of feeling—the absence of the feeling of God's presence during prayer.

Several of the great spiritual masters have written extensively on this topic, especially St. Teresa of Ávila and St. John of the Cross. In *An Introduction to the Devout Life*, St. Francis de Sales deals with the topic only briefly by offering some practical advice.

The first is that we should not become disheartened if we experience dryness or let it be an excuse not to pray. He suggests that if we find dryness in mental prayer, we should try vocal prayer (prayer spoken aloud) or spiritual reading. "Take a book," the saint advises, "and read attentively until your mind is quickened and reassured." He also suggests using bodily posture or gestures to stir ourselves to ardor, such as making prostrations or embracing a crucifix. But if none of these remedies work, he says, "do not be disheartened, only continue to present yourself devoutly before God" (2, 9).

We must remember that we don't pray because it gives us good feelings. If good feelings come to us while we pray, we should count them as a blessing. But prayer is not any less virtuous without them. Religious emotion comes more easily to some than to others. As St. John Henry Newman observed, "The natural tempers of men vary very much. Some men have ardent imaginations and strong feelings.... Their ardor does not of itself make their faith deeper and more genuine."[48]

In his other writings, St. Francis de Sales reminds us that we pray for two principal reasons. "The first is to render to God the honor and homage which we owe him," and "The second ... is to speak to him, and to hear him speak to us by his inspirations and interior motions.... One of these reasons may sometimes fail us, but both never."[49]

People will sometimes wonder that they never hear God speak to them in prayer. God does not normally speak to us in audible words. While some mystics have received audible locutions from God, these miracles are exceedingly rare! The usual way God communicates to us in prayer is through movements of the heart or by imparting images or ideas to our mind. If we desire to hear God's word more directly, we have only to read the Scriptures.

God is a good Father who gives His children what they need. If we need spiritual consolation to assure us of His presence, He will grant that to us. But He also grants periods of dryness so that we may learn not to rely on "good feelings" as a substitute for true faith. St. Francis cautions that "we must distinguish between God and a perception of God, between faith and a feeling of faith."[50]

Another obstacle everyone encounters in prayer is distraction. Rather than offer suggestions on how to overcome distraction, St. Francis says we shouldn't be distracted by distraction!

---

[48] Newman, *Parochial and Plain Sermons*, Sermon 14.
[49] *Consoling Thoughts of St. Francis de Sales: On Trials of an Interior Life*, comp. Père Huguet (Charlotte, NC: TAN Books, 2013), 58–59.
[50] Ibid., 61.

The least trifle of a distraction cannot withdraw your soul from God, since nothing withdraws us from God but sin.... Even venial sins are not capable of turning us aside from the way which conducts to God; they undoubtedly retard us a little on our course, but they do not turn us aside: much less simple distractions.[51]

One unseasonably warm autumn morning, I thought I would pray outside by the creek running through our backyard. I thought I could get away from the noise of children playing in my home and pray my Rosary without distraction. I wasn't halfway through the first decade when I heard a buzzing by my feet. An injured cicada was crawling on the ground and being attacked by a wasp. I tried to meditate on the mysteries, but I couldn't help getting caught up in this miniature nature documentary playing out before my eyes—especially when the dying cicada began crawling in my direction, bringing his wasp assailant with him! So much for my attempts to pray free from distraction.

The truth is, we bring distractions with us wherever we go—even if we were to pray in a sensory-deprivation chamber; our biggest distractions come from within our own minds. Over time, through discipline, we can learn to focus our minds despite distractions, but we will never be entirely free of them—at least not in this life. And if we become too concerned with being free of distractions, that in itself can become a great distraction. If we are focused on not being distracted, we are not focused on God.

St. Francis warns against overthinking or being too self-aware in prayer. He wants our prayer to be simple. "Would you wish to behold God?" St. Francis writes. "Behold him then, and be

---

[51]   Ibid., 60-61.

attentive to that; for if you begin to reflect and examine how you look to yourself while you are looking on him, it is no longer God you are viewing, but yourself."[52]

Our prayer is not rendered any less agreeable to God by dryness or distraction. These are obstacles only to us — not to Him. In fact, if we faithfully persist in prayer despite these seeming obstacles, we can be assured that we do so out of love of God rather than a love of His gifts.

[52] Ibid., 62.

## Questions for Reflection

1. Have you experienced times of dryness in prayer? Have you found any helpful ways to overcome it?
2. What things distract you during mental prayer? How have you attempted to address those distractions?
3. How might St. Francis's assurance that dryness and distractions do not make our prayer any less worthy affect your perception of prayer?

## Scripture for Meditation

My God, my God, why have you abandoned me?
Why so far from my call for help,
from my cries of anguish?
My God, I call by day, but you do not answer;
by night, but I have no relief.
Yet you are enthroned as the Holy One;
you are the glory of Israel. (Ps. 22:2–4)

# 7

# The Sacred Liturgy

The Second Vatican Council calls the Eucharist "the source and summit of the Christian life."[53] It is the foundation of our Faith and its pinnacle. It is the depth and the height, the Alpha and Omega. How could the Eucharist not be at the center of the devout life? St. Francis de Sales refers to it as "the center of the Christian religion, the heart of devotion, the soul of piety," an "ineffable mystery which embraces the untold depths of divine charity" in which God gives Himself freely to us. Our prayer when united with the Divine Sacrifice of the Mass, St. Francis attests, has "unutterable power." Therefore, he encourages us to "be present daily at Holy Mass" as often as possible, to offer the sacrifice of Christ "together with the priest" both on our own behalf and on behalf of the Church (2, 14).

By this brief exhortation, St. Francis brings to light two often overlooked aspects of the liturgy. The first is the important role that each of us plays in the corporate prayer of the Church. The Mass is not the sacrifice of the priest. It is the Church's participation in the one sacrifice of Christ, the High Priest, offered by the presiding priest in union with the lay faithful by virtue of our common baptismal priesthood. This is attested to in the Eucharistic Liturgy when the priest addresses the congregation, saying, "Pray, brethren, that my sacrifice *and yours* may be acceptable to God, the almighty Father."[54]

---

[53] *LG* 11.
[54] *Roman Missal*, 3rd ed., emphasis added.

The second important reminder is that our participation in this sacrifice is not for our personal benefit only. The faithful respond to the priest's invitation by saying, "May the Lord accept the sacrifice at your hands for the praise and glory of his name, for our good *and the good of all his holy Church.*"[55] We have a solemn duty to attend Mass not only for our own good but for the spiritual benefit of the entire Christian community—and indeed the whole world.

This is why participation in Mass on Sundays and holy days is not optional. It is not one spiritual practice among many that we can choose to observe or not. It is our obligation (and our privilege) as members of the Body of Christ to join in the sacrifice of Christ, the Head on behalf of the Body—a Body that includes more members than those visible to us. At every Mass, we are in the company of the angels and saints who join their prayers to ours. As St. Francis acclaims, "What a privilege to be united in so blessed and mighty an action!" (2, 14).

We sometimes speak of "attending" Mass as we might attend the theater or a sporting event. But the Mass is not a spectator sport. It is not something to be observed passively as entertainment. The word *liturgy* originally meant a public work, or work done on behalf of the people (CCC 1069). The Church applies this term to our public prayer because prayer is work, and as work, it is something we should be actively engaged in.

Previous generations of Catholics spoke of "assisting" at Mass. This underscores the role we all have in assisting the priest by our prayer. Even the more common expression of "attending" Mass speaks to this truth if we know what it means to be attentive. To *attend* means "to be present at," not only in body but also in mind

---

[55] Ibid., emphasis added.

and spirit. The word comes from the Latin *ad tendere*, which means "to stretch." Prayerful participation at Mass should stretch us a bit.

The Second Vatican Council calls for the faithful to participate in the Mass "intelligently, actively and fruitfully."[56] As Mass begins, St. Francis de Sales says, "place yourself in the presence of God, acknowledging your unworthiness, and asking pardon for your faults" (2, 14). Throughout Mass, you should meditate upon the life and work of Christ. And as Mass ends, you should thank God and humbly ask for His blessings for yourself, your family and friends, and the whole Church. Indeed, the prayers of the Mass call us to do these very things if we are mindful of them.

Although St. Francis de Sales encourages daily participation in the Mass, depending on your circumstances and station in life, this may not be practical or possible. Do what you can, always observing the canonical requirement to participate in Mass at least on Sundays and on holy days of obligation.[57] Even participating in Mass one or two days during the week in addition to Sunday is of great spiritual benefit! When you cannot be present at Mass on any given day, St. Francis suggests making a spiritual communion, uniting your prayerful intentions to those of the Church and offering the same spiritual service as you would if you were physically present.[58]

St. Francis also points out the importance of liturgical prayer outside the Mass. The ongoing, daily prayer of the Church is the Liturgy of the Hours, also known as the Divine Office. It is the Church's way of sanctifying time by praying in common at certain hours "to sanctify the day and the whole range of human activity."[59]

---

[56] Second Vatican Council, Constitution on the Sacred Liturgy *Sacrosanctum Concilium* (SC) (December 4, 1963), no. 11.

[57] Can. 1247.

[58] You can find an Act of Spiritual Communion in part 2, chapter 11.

[59] *General Instruction of the Liturgy of the Hours*, 11.

# The Devout Life

Consisting primarily of psalms and prayers of petition, the Church calls the Liturgy of the Hours "the voice of the Bride speaking to the Bridegroom, or rather, the prayer of Christ with his Body to the Father."[60] As such, it is especially suited to a life of devotion, and this is why clergy and those in religious life have a special mandate to pray the office faithfully and why lay faithful have always been drawn to participate in this prayer as much as they are able. Many popular Catholic devotions have their origins in the lay faithful's desire to pray in connection with the Divine Office. The Rosary, for example, is sometimes called "Our Lady's Psalter" because its 153 recitations of the Hail Mary (the five decades of each of the three traditional sets of mysteries, plus the three of the introductory prayers) originate in the 153 psalms prayed in the monastic office. The Angelus is traditionally prayed at six o'clock in the morning, noon, and six o'clock in the evening because that is when the church bells would ring to summon the monks to their prayers. At the sound of their tolling, the faithful would momentarily pause their work to join their prayers with those of the Church.

St. Francis recommends, "Assist in the Divine Office as much as you are able," especially "on Sundays and festivals" (2, 15). This is echoed in the Second Vatican Council's call for pastors to offer public celebrations of the hours at least on Sundays and feast days.[61] Alas, this aspiration of the Council remains unrealized in most Catholic parishes. Even so, other advances have made the Liturgy of the Hours more accessible than ever. Affordable, single-volume editions of *Christian Prayer* enable anyone to participate in the daily prayer of the Church, no matter where they are. Divine Office

---

[60]  SC 84.
[61]  SC 100.

apps for smartphones and tablet devices are becoming increasingly popular. (The downside to using electronic devices to pray is that they frequently are also sources of distraction.)

Whether you pray the Liturgy of the Hours in community or alone, it is liturgical prayer, and that means that you are participating in the public prayer of the Church. As important as it is to foster personal prayer in your life of devotion, St. Francis declares "once and for all, there is always more benefit and consolation to be derived from the public offices of the Church than from private particular acts. God has ordained that communion in prayer must always be preferred to every form of private prayer" (2, 15).

## Questions for Reflection

1. Do you sometimes find it difficult to pay attention at Mass? What might you do to remain focused and be more prayerfully engaged in the liturgy?
2. Is it practical or possible for you to attend Mass more frequently than you do? If not, what other ways might you increase your participation in the public prayer of the Church, such as the Liturgy of the Hours?
3. Why would St. Francis say there is more benefit in participating in the public prayer of the Church than in private prayer? What do you gain from public liturgy that cannot be found in private devotion?

## Scripture for Meditation

They devoted themselves to the teaching of the apostles and to the communal life, to the breaking of the bread and to the prayers.... Every day they devoted themselves to meeting in the temple area and to breaking bread in their homes. They ate their meals with exultation and sincerity of heart, praising God and enjoying favor with all the people. (Acts 2:42, 46–47)

8

# Heavenly Friends

The last chapter dealt with liturgy as the corporate prayer of the entire Church. But the Church includes more members than those who are visible to us in this world. The Body of Christ extends into Heaven and includes the angels and the saints.

The word *angel* means "messenger." The role of these spiritual beings is to serve as divine messengers, heralds of good news, and ambassadors of grace. We see this in the angel Gabriel's annunciation to Mary: "The angel Gabriel was sent from God ... to a virgin betrothed to a man named Joseph" (Luke 1:26–27). Gabriel also delivered God's message to Joseph in a dream (Matt. 1:20) and His message to the priest Zechariah during his liturgical service in the temple (Luke 1:11). Sometimes God's messengers appear to us in human form, as did Raphael to Tobias (Tob. 5:4) and the three angels who visited Abraham (Gen. 18:1–15).

St. Francis de Sales reminds us that these divine couriers carry messages in both directions. "Since God often sends us His inspirations by means of His angels, we ought frequently to offer Him our aspirations through the same channel" (2, 16). At the Annunciation, Gabriel's angelic role was not only to deliver God's message to Mary but to receive her response and carry it back to God. "Mary said, 'Behold, I am the handmaid of the Lord. May it be done to me according to your word.' Then the angel departed from her" (Luke 1:38).

We might think that only important figures in salvation history, such as Abraham and Mary, are visited by angels, but the

*Catechism* instructs us, "Beside each believer stands an angel as protector and shepherd leading him to life" (336). Many adult Catholics today sadly make no effort to implore the aid of these powerful spiritual guardians given to us by God for our benefit and protection. Many treat guardian angels as objects of childish fantasy. Just as adults stop believing in the Easter Bunny and the tooth fairy, many Catholics cease to believe in their guardian angels as they leave childhood behind. This is a grave mistake! Guardian angels are not fairy tales or stories told to calm scared children. Jesus Himself attests to the reality of guardian angels when He says, "See that you do not despise one of these little ones, for I say to you that their angels in heaven always look upon the face of my heavenly Father" (Matt. 18:10).

Christ teaches explicitly that our angels always behold the face of God. That means they experience the Beatific Vision even as they watch over us. They experience now what we hope to experience in Heaven. To do this, they must be powerfully holy beings. Looking upon the face of God is no small matter. When Moses asked to see God's glory, God told him, "You cannot see my face, for no man can see me and live" (Exod. 33:20). Yet our angels see God's face continuously.

Because our guardian angels always have both us and God in their sight, they serve as important conduits between us and the divine. They simultaneously see both where we are now and the goal we journey toward; they are therefore uniquely suited to help us reach our destination. It would be foolish not to befriend your guardian angel. No one else, other than Christ Himself, desires as much to get you into Heaven. Your angel is truly your best friend and most trusted protector.

We should also be mindful that everyone around us has an angelic protector, and we should seek their intercession as we pray for our friends and loved ones. St. Francis implores, "Familiarize yourself with the thought of holy angels, and honor especially the angel guardian of the diocese in which you live, and those of your neighbors, and above all your own. Call on them and honor them frequently, and ask their help in all your affairs, temporal as well as spiritual" (2, 16).

About angels, the great abbot St. Bernard of Clairvaux remarks:

> Even though we are children and have a long, a very long and dangerous way to go, with such protectors what have we to fear? They who keep us in all our ways cannot be overpowered or led astray, much less lead us astray. They are loyal, prudent, powerful. Why then are we afraid? We have only to follow them, stay close to them, and we shall dwell under the protection of God's heaven.[62]

Angels are not our only heavenly friends. We also have the saints, our brothers and sisters in Christ who have gone before us in faith, to serve as our examples and to intercede on our behalf. St. Francis says, "Choose as your patrons some saints in particular, to whose life and imitation you feel most drawn, and in whose intercession you feel an especial confidence. The saint whose name you bear is already assigned you from your Baptism" (2, 16).

Your reasons for adopting any given saint as a patron are entirely yours. It may be because you bear the name of that saint, as St. Francis mentions. Or perhaps you were born on that saint's feast day. You may develop a devotion to a saint who is the patron of your occupation or of a particular interest or need of yours or whose spiritual writings you find especially helpful. Relationships

---

[62] Quoted in the Office of Readings, memorial of the Guardian Angels.

with saints are like any other friendship; they happen naturally as we encounter the saints and get to know them better.

To this end, St. Francis de Sales recommends that we always have some good spiritual writings from the saints at hand to read from daily, "counting them as letters from ... heaven intended to show you the road thither and give you courage to follow it. Also study the lives of the saints, in which you will behold a portrait of the true Christian's life as in a mirror, and you can adapt their examples to your own life" (2, 17).

To be a Christian is to have the Spirit of Christ in you (Rom. 8:9). It is to be formed in Christ's likeness and thus bring to perfection the image of God in which you were made. The saints have accomplished this. They therefore serve not only as intercessors but also as models. They can direct us along the path to Heaven because they have walked the road before us; they know how to navigate the obstacles and pitfalls along the way.

Among all the saints, none has conformed herself to the likeness of Christ more than His Blessed Mother. St. Francis writes that we should

honor, reverence, and love the holy and glorious Virgin Mary, for she is the Mother of Our Lord, and therefore our Mother also. Fly to her as a child, and cast yourself at her knees with a perfect confidence at all times, and on all occasions. Call on this dear Mother, appeal to her maternal love, and strive to imitate her virtues. (2, 16)

## Questions for Reflection

1. When was the last time you prayed to your guardian angel, either asking for his intercession or thanking him for his aid? What would it mean to have a relationship with your guardian angel now?

2. Are there saints you have a special relationship with or have adopted as patrons? In what ways have you been aware of their intercession in your life?

3. How do Mary and the other saints serve as models for you in your daily life? In prayer, work, school, family relationships, and friendships, how do they inspire you to be more Christlike?

## Scripture for Meditation

Another angel came and stood at the altar, holding a gold censer. He was given a great quantity of incense to offer, along with the prayers of all the holy ones, on the gold altar that was before the throne. The smoke of the incense along with the prayers of the holy ones went up before God from the hand of the angel. (Rev. 8:3-4)

# 9

# Receiving Inspiration

The word *inspire* means "to breathe into," from the Latin word *spiritus*, from which we also get the word *spirit*. When God inspires us, He breathes His Spirit into us. It is what we ask for when we pray, "Come, Holy Spirit."

God's Spirit is what gives us life. "The LORD God formed the man out of the dust of the ground and blew into his nostrils the breath of life, and the man became a living being" (Gen. 2:7). God's Spirit also gives us new life through the forgiveness of sins. "He breathed on them and said to them, 'Receive the Holy Spirit. Whose sins you forgive are forgiven them, and whose sins you retain are retained'" (John 20:22–23). This same Spirit sustains us in our life of devotion. It is important, therefore, to learn how to hear and respond to the promptings of the Spirit.

We often talk of God "speaking to us" in prayer, but (except for miraculous audible locutions) God doesn't speak in ways discernible to our external senses. The Spirit is subtle. St. Francis de Sales describes inspirations as "the affections, attractions, inward reproaches and regrets, perceptions and illuminations with which God moves us."[63]

When a friend sitting across the room speaks to you, it is a physical action. Air escapes his lungs, causing vibrations that reverberate in your ears. You can tell who is speaking, and what

---

[63] Quotations in the chapter are taken from part 2, chapter 18.

direction the voice is coming from. When a spiritual person (such as God, His angel messengers, or one of the fallen angels) wishes to communicate with you, it is an entirely different matter. He has no lungs, no tongue, no vocal chords. His words have no physical impact. They may not be words at all, according to our understanding of the term. We do not "hear" these words because they operate not upon our eardrums but rather directly upon our minds. We receive spiritual communication in the spiritual part of our being as the affections and perceptions that St. Francis de Sales describes.

Have you ever had a thought pop into your head seemingly from nowhere? Well, it might not be from nowhere. It could be the prompting of your guardian angel. It may be a distraction or temptation of the devil. And of course, it could simply be the product of your mind.

We may wonder why God's inspirations would be so hard to hear and so easy to ignore. Wouldn't the Almighty God proclaim His message with trumpet blasts and fanfare? We may think so, but God's ways are not our ways. Consider God's revelation to Elijah (1 Kings 19:11–13). God spoke not in the wind, the earthquake, or the fire, but in the "still small voice" (RSVCE) that Elijah could easily have missed if he was not listening for it. God is a gentleman. He leaves room for our cooperation. Most often He prompts rather than demands. He invites rather than insists. He speaks to those willing to listen. If we are not open to His inspiration, we will not receive it, dismissing it instead as a fleeting thought or a passing notion.

Being attentive to the inner promptings of the Spirit requires careful discernment on our part. Fallen angels can similarly "inspire" us with their diabolical impressions. St. Francis warns, "When the enemy sees a soul ready to consent to inspirations, he often seeks to deceive it." As we draw closer to God, we become more tempting targets for the devil. When we are far from God, we don't warrant Satan's attention because we are already where he wants us to be. By his evil inspirations, he will attempt to deceive us, tempt us, and cause us to doubt God's mercy and love. If any apparent inspiration we receive goes against Church teaching, contradicts Scripture, leads us to disobey rightful authority, or causes us to doubt the Faith, we can be sure it is of the devil. We should reject these devious suggestions as soon as they come and not give them further thought.

Inspirations from God may not always "feel good." They can comfort and console us, but they can also admonish and reproach us. In all cases, they will call us to a greater degree of holiness. Likewise, Satan's inspirations may not always "feel bad." The easiest way to lead us into evil is to convince us that it's really good ("Did God *really say* you shall not eat from the fruit of the tree ...? [see Gen. 3:1]) or tempt us to choose a lesser good over a greater one. Lucifer (the light bearer) is an angel of light, after all. His temptations wouldn't be tempting if they were not attractive. But they will always seek to lead us away from God, Christ, the Church, and true, selfless charity. The different tenors of angelic and demonic inspiration become easier to discern with experience. When in doubt, an objective third-party perspective can be invaluable, so St. Francis advises consultation with your spiritual director before acting upon your inspirations "in any important or unusual matters."

And act upon them we must. Receiving God's inspiration benefits us only if we respond to it. St. Francis de Sales likens God's inspiration to a marriage proposal made by a lover to his beloved. First the beloved hears the proposal. This is what happens when we receive inspiration from God. Next, the proposal causes the beloved to feel a certain way; perhaps pleased, perhaps offended, perhaps fearful, depending on her attitude toward her suitor. And so God's inspiration may cause us to feel differently, depending on our openness to His will. But no matter how the proposal makes the beloved feel, she is not betrothed until she gives her consent. The point of her good feeling is to make her yes come more easily, but good feeling alone is not sufficient. This is the third and final step in receiving God's inspiration: we must respond with an act of the will. We must do what God is calling us to do. We must give our *fiat* not only in word but in deed.

"The perfection lies in consent," St. Francis writes. "Consent in the heart producing no outward results is like a vine that bears no fruit." The specific resolutions St. Francis advises us to make as part of our daily prayer, described earlier in this section, are a very useful tool in this regard, as the purpose of them is to lead us to concrete actions in response to the Spirit's prompting, which we are most open to hearing during our daily prayer.

## Questions for Reflection

1. When filling out our contact information on forms, we are often asked, "What is the best way to reach you?" What is the best way for God to reach you? How can you most easily hear His voice during prayer? At other times during the day? Are you listening for His call?

2. In the above example, the beloved might receive her suitor's proposal with feelings of pleasure, fear, or offense. How does this compare with your experience of hearing God in prayer? Do you perceive God's voice more often as a comfort or an admonishment?

3. Do you find it challenging to connect the inspirations received in prayer to your daily life? Why might it be difficult at times to put inspiration into action, and what can we do to respond more faithfully and fruitfully to God's call?

## Scripture for Meditation

I was sleeping, but my heart was awake.
The sound of my lover knocking!
"Open to me, my sister, my friend,
my dove, my perfect one!" (Song of Songs 5:2)

May it be done to me according to your word. (Luke 1:38)

# 10

# Confession

One aspect of Jesus' ministry that most directly attests to His divinity is the forgiveness of sins. When our Lord told the paralytic, "Your sins are forgiven," the scribes said, "He is blaspheming. Who but God alone can forgive sins?" They recognized that forgiveness is divine but failed to recognize the divinity of the Forgiver. "But that you may know that the Son of Man has authority to forgive sins on earth," Jesus healed the paralytic man (Mark 2:5-7, 10-11).

The One who possessed the authority to forgive sins passed that authority on to His Church. He told the Apostles, "As the Father has sent me, so I send you." He then breathed on them, saying, "Receive the Holy Spirit. Whose sins you forgive are forgiven them, and whose sins you retain are retained" (John 20:21-23).

Given that Christ has entrusted the Church with such a divine gift, how foolish would we be not to take advantage of it! St. Francis de Sales says, "Since then you have so sure and simple a remedy at hand, never permit your heart to remain long sullied by sin.... Why should we die a spiritual death, since we have so sovereign a remedy?"[64]

As I mentioned in chapter 5 of part 1, even after initial conversion and rebirth in Baptism, we continue to struggle with sin. A life of devotion is a life of ongoing conversion requiring a daily decision to die to self and live for Christ. The grace available

---

[64] Quotations in this chapter are taken from part 2, chapter 19.

through sacramental Confession not only restores us to divine life when we fall into mortal sin; it also heals the wounds caused by venial sin and strengthens us in our work of ongoing conversion.

A word about mortal versus venial sin: As St. John puts it, "All wrongdoing is sin, but there is sin that is not deadly" (1 John 5:17). Mortal, or deadly, sin "destroys charity in the heart of man by a grave violation of God's law" (CCC 1855). This is possible not because sin is stronger than God's grace, but because God, in His love, always respects our free will. He invites us to love Him and share in His life, but we are free to reject His invitation. If we were not free, then accepting His invitation would not be an act of love.

To commit a mortal sin is to engage in behavior that is incompatible with the life of God. It is as if God says to us, "You are free to do this thing you are considering, but it is contrary to my nature. If you choose to go there, I cannot go with you." Or as St. Paul puts it, "If we are unfaithful he remains faithful, for he cannot deny himself" (2 Tim. 2:13).

To be guilty of mortal sin, therefore, three conditions must be true: the act itself must be gravely wrong, we must know that it is wrong, and we must freely choose it.[65] We may not consciously be rejecting God by our sin, but the effect is still the same. By choosing to do something incompatible with the life of God, even when we know better, we tell God that we prefer our will to His.

Any sin that does not meet all three of those conditions *is still a sin*, but it is not contrary to the life of God because it does not derive from a (conscious or unconscious) rejection of God's love. We call this sin *venial*, meaning "excusable." It derives not from a rejection of God's love but from the human weakness we all experience as a result of the Fall, even after our conversion. Although

[65] CCC 1857–1860.

sacramental confession is necessary for "those who have fallen into grave [mortal] sin, and have thus lost their baptismal grace," the "confession of everyday faults (venial sins) is nevertheless strongly recommended by the Church" (CCC 1446, 1458).

St. Francis de Sales recommends frequent confession of even venial sins because, by it, "you not only receive absolution from the venial sins you confess but also great strength to avoid them in the future, light to see them clearly, and abundant grace to repair whatever damage you have incurred."[66] For anyone seeking to grow in devotion, confession should be frequent, sincere, and specific.

How frequent? Church law requires that we confess at least once per year.[67] But the minimum required by law is not the ideal practice of devotion. St. Francis de Sales recommends Confession "once a week, always if possible before receiving Holy Communion." Frequent confession of venial sins allows us to engage in the fine work of spiritual growth—not only rooting out the thorns of mortal sin but also pulling up the weeds of fault and weakness and addressing the underlying conditions that cause them to grow in our hearts. By frequently confessing even venial sins on a regular schedule, "you practice the virtues of humility, obedience, simplicity, and love, so that by the act of confession you exercise more virtues than by any other means."

While our confessions should be regular, they should also be sincere. St. Francis warns against letting them become automatic. We ought to truly detest our sins and have the desire to do better. If we have no resolution at least to attempt to amend our faults, we are not taking full advantage of the graces available to us in the sacrament. St. Francis speaks poorly of those who confess

---

[66] Ryan translation.
[67] Can. 989.

"mechanically and from habit" with no resolution to change, saying they "lose much spiritual good."

Our confessions should also be specific. St. Francis warns us to avoid generalities, such as "I have not loved God as I ought" or "I have not shown charity toward my neighbor." Once I confessed to my pastor, "My prayer life is not what it should be." He chortled and said, "Whose is?" Confessing generic imperfections that we all have, St. Francis says, doesn't tell our confessor anything useful about the state of our conscience, "since all the Saints now in Paradise, and every living being might confess the same." We need to dig deeper and look for the specific reasons we have for accusing ourselves of these faults. If you have been neglectful in prayer, in what way? Why? Have you been distracted? Are you prioritizing lesser things over your duties to God? Have you been wasteful in how you use your time? If you have not been charitable to your neighbor, in what way has this manifested itself? Did you see your neighbor in need and fail to help him? Did you spread gossip about him? Have you borne a grudge against him for some perceived insult? Be specific.

St. Francis advises us to also confess "the motive which induced the sin." Did I fail to help my neighbor because of anger, indifference, or laziness? Have I neglected my prayers out of forgetfulness or out of a lack of zeal? Likewise, we should mention the duration of our sin. How long has this fault persisted? "There is a wide difference," he observes, "between the passing vanity which surprised us for a quarter of an hour, and that which has engrossed our heart for a day or more."

The more open, honest, and specific we can be about our sins, the better our confessor will know how to heal our spiritual wounds. Regular and frequent Confession is an indispensable tool for growth in sanctity as we model our lives more and more on the life of the Savior. For this reason, St. Francis says you should "not lightly change your confessor; but having selected one be punctual in opening your conscience to him at the appointed times, telling him simply and honestly all your faults."

## Questions for Reflection

1. Have the reflections in part 1 of this book made a difference in your participation in the sacrament of Confession? How so? Has that led to other changes in your spiritual life?
2. What makes mortal sin "deadly" and venial sin "excusable"? Are there sins that you perhaps considered venial in the past that you realize now may have been mortal sins? And vice versa?
3. The last chapter discussed the importance of putting inspiration into action. How does this coincide with the call to repentance and reconciliation in Confession?

## Scripture for Meditation

So whoever is in Christ is a new creation: the old things have passed away; behold, new things have come. And all this is from God, who has reconciled us to himself through Christ and given us the ministry of reconciliation, namely, God was reconciling the world to himself in Christ, not counting their trespasses against them and entrusting to us the message of reconciliation. So we are ambassadors for Christ, as if God were appealing through us. We implore you on behalf of Christ, be reconciled to God. (2 Cor. 5:17–20)

# 11

# Communion

Jesus first spoke of the Eucharist the day after He performed the miracle of the multiplication of the loaves and fishes. He told the crowd, who had gathered in hopes of having their bellies fed once more, "My flesh is true food, and my blood is true drink. Whoever eats my flesh and drinks my blood remains in me and I in him." After hearing this, the Gospel says, "many of his disciples ... no longer accompanied him." Only the apostles remained, those who had "come to believe" (John 6:55–56, 66, 69). Ever since then, the Eucharist has been the focal point of devotion to Christ, who took bread, gave thanks, broke it, and said, "This is my body" (Luke 22:19).

All devotion to Jesus must ultimately be Eucharistic because the Eucharist *is Jesus* – Body, Blood, Soul, and Divinity. Yet it appears to our senses as mere bread and wine. In the middle of the second century, St. Justin Martyr wrote about this mystery:

> We do not receive these things as common bread or common drink; but in like manner as Jesus Christ our Savior having been incarnate by God's logos took both flesh and blood for our salvation, so also we have been taught that the food eucharistized through the word of prayer that is from him, from which our blood and flesh are nourished by transformation, is the flesh and blood of that Jesus who became incarnate. [68]

[68]  *First Apology* 66.

This is one of the most mind-bogglingly beautiful teachings of our Faith. God loves us so much that He not only became one of us but became *food for us*, so that He might dwell within us in body as well as in spirit. The most understandable reason for not believing in the Eucharist is that it's too good to be true. And yet it is true. As St. Francis attests, "There is nothing in which the love of Christ is set forth more tenderly or more touchingly than in this Sacrament, by which he, so to say, annihilates himself for us, and takes upon him the form of bread, in order to feed us, and unite himself closely to the bodies and souls of the faithful" (2, 21).

The Eucharist provides spiritual nourishment for the daily trials of our pilgrimage on earth, as the *Catechism* explains:

What material food produces in our bodily life, Holy Communion wonderfully achieves in our spiritual life.... This growth in Christian life needs the nourishment of Eucharistic Communion, the bread for our pilgrimage until the moment of death, when it will be given to us as viaticum.... As bodily nourishment restores lost strength, so the Eucharist strengthens our charity, which tends to be weakened in daily life. (1392, 1394)

St. Francis de Sales also speaks of the Eucharist as protection, saying:

He who frequently and devoutly feeds [upon the Eucharist] so strengthens the life and health of his soul that it can scarcely be poisoned by any evil passions....

If the most delicate and perishable fruits ... can easily be preserved the whole year by means of sugar or honey, surely it is no great marvel that our hearts, albeit frail and weak, should be preserved from the corruption of sin when they are immersed in the sweetness of the incorruptible Body and Blood of the Son of God (2, 20).

Although St. Francis strongly recommends assisting at daily Mass if possible (see part 2, chapter 7 of this book), he is more hesitant to recommend daily Communion. "I neither exhort you to receive the Blessed Sacrament daily, nor do I forbid it," he writes. "But I do exhort every one to communicate at least every Sunday, if his heart be pure from affection to sin" (2, 20). This underscores the distinction between our obligation to give corporate worship to God, primarily by assisting in the Liturgy of the Mass, and the reception of Holy Communion. The former is a duty; the latter is a gift. The law of the Church mandates that Catholics should receive Communion at least once a year, during the Easter Season,[69] but St. Francis observes that "no one who really desires to seek God in the devout life" should receive Communion less than once per month (2, 20). We cannot grow in devotion by settling for the minimal observance of the Faith!

But St. Francis is more concerned that we receive the Eucharist properly rather than frequently. It was a matter of concern for him, writing five centuries ago, to encourage people to receive at least once a month. He provides words of counsel to those who fear they may be judged by others if they receive Communion too often. Today we have the opposite problem, with even nominal Catholics routinely receiving Communion every time they are at Mass, without giving any thought to the state of their souls.

This is important. The Eucharist is the Bread of Life, and receiving the sacrament worthily is a matter of (spiritual) life or death. St. Paul warns that "whoever eats the bread or drinks the cup of the

[69] CCC 2042; CIC 920.

Lord unworthily ... eats and drinks judgment on himself" (1 Cor. 11:27–29). What does it mean to receive the Eucharist worthily? Are any of us worthy of God? No. Union with God is possible only by God's free gift of Himself to us. To receive Communion worthily, we must not have rejected God's gift through mortal sin (see the previous chapter). To receive the Eucharist worthily is to receive it *honestly*. To receive Communion, we should *be in Communion* with God and with the Church. Mortal sin breaks that communion. To receive Communion in that state is to turn what should be an act of love into a lie. We eat and drink judgment on ourselves. Before receiving Communion, we must therefore examine our consciences and, if necessary, be reconciled with God through Confession. God's mercy is limitless; we have only to ask for it. To refuse to do so is to say to God, "I want communion with You on *my terms*, not Yours."

Even in a state of grace, we must still approach the altar with utmost humility and gratitude, praying, "Lord, I am not worthy that you should enter under my roof, but only say the word and my soul shall be healed."[70]

Every reception of the Eucharist is a cause for celebration. However often we receive, it should be something we look forward to. St. Francis advises to "begin the evening before to prepare yourself for Holy Communion by many aspirations and movements of love, retiring a little earlier, in order that you may be able to rise earlier next morning."[71] We should be mindful to observe the Eucharistic fast for at least an hour before Communion to prepare our bodies and should dress properly and carry ourselves so that our demeanor "convey[s] the respect, solemnity, and joy of this moment when

---

[70] *Roman Missal*, cf. Matt. 8:8.
[71] Ross translation.

Christ becomes our guest" (CCC 1387). St. Francis implores us, after receiving Communion, to "give [Jesus] the best welcome that you can, and let it be seen by the holiness of all your actions that God is with you.... Your chief aim in Holy Communion should be to advance, strengthen, and comfort yourself in the love of God; receiving for love's sake, what love alone can give" (2, 21).

If there are times when you are unable to receive the Eucharist—perhaps even for some time—due to illness, the absence of a priest, or other circumstances beyond your control, do not despair. Remember that God made the sacraments for our benefit, but He Himself is not bound by them. His grace is always available in our need. "When you are unable actually to receive him in the Holy Eucharist," St. Francis advises, "then unite yourself by the earnestness of your desires to this life-giving flesh of the Saviour, and communicate spiritually in your heart" (2, 21).

### ACT OF SPIRITUAL COMMUNION

*My Jesus, I believe that You are present in the Most Holy Sacrament. I love You above all things, and I desire to receive You into my soul. Since I cannot at this moment receive You sacramentally, come at least spiritually into my heart. I embrace You as if You were already there and unite myself wholly to You. Never permit me to be separated from You. Amen.*

## Questions for Reflection

1. Do you routinely receive Communion without thought every time you go to Mass? Or do you do so only after having made a careful examination of conscience with due consideration of your spiritual state?
2. Have you ever been away from the Eucharist? What effect did that have on your spiritual life? How did it feel to receive the Eucharist again after that absence?
3. Have you ever been aware of the Eucharist strengthening you for spiritual battle or protecting you from evil influence? How was this manifested in your life?

## Scripture for Meditation

[Jesus] went in to stay with them. And it happened that, while he was with them at table, he took bread, said the blessing, broke it, and gave it to them. With that their eyes were opened and they recognized him, but he vanished from their sight.... So they set out at once and returned to Jerusalem.... Then the two recounted what had taken place on the way and how he was made known to them in the breaking of the bread. (Luke 24:29–35)

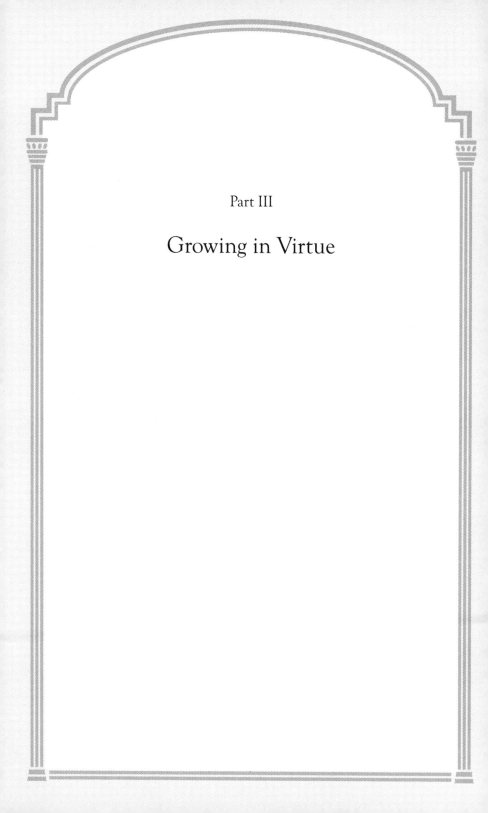

Part III

# Growing in Virtue

1

# Choosing Virtue

What does it mean to be a good person? The qualities we associate with moral goodness in a person are called virtues, from the Latin word *vir*, meaning "man." The ancient Romans conceived of virtues as manly qualities to be prized in soldiers, but the concept soon developed beyond this narrow view to encompass the universal concept of *virtus*, describing the upright moral qualities of men, women and children, noblemen and slaves, and everyone in between. All people are capable of being good, and virtues are those qualities of goodness.

But did not our Lord say, "No one is good but God alone" (Mark 10:18)? It is true that all goodness originates in God, but as a creature made in God's image (Gen. 1:27), man is capable of reflecting the goodness of the Creator. It's what we were made to do. As St. Ireneaus observes, "The glory of God is man fully alive."[72] To be a *good man* means to be like God. To be a *bad man* is to be unlike God. The *best man* is the most like God, and for our model of virtue God gives us the *perfect man*, Jesus Christ, who calls us to divine perfection (Matt. 5:48). To be virtuous, therefore, is to be like Jesus, which is the very definition of holiness. This makes the pursuit of virtue a necessary part of living a devout life.

But we can't just aim for virtue generically. That would be like going to school to learn "knowledge." You can't just learn

---

[72] *Against Heresies* 4, 20.

"knowledge." You have to choose a subject. You must focus your mental efforts on studying history, mathematics, or science in order to grow in those specific areas of knowledge. Virtue is the same way. Wanting to grow in virtue is good—but which virtue? And how does one grow in it?

St. Francis de Sales teaches us to be practical in choosing which virtues to focus on. Some virtues are required of us more frequently than others. For example, most of us will only rarely have the need for courage. "But every action of our daily life," he writes, "should be influenced by gentleness, temperance, humility and purity."[73] It would be wise for us to master those virtues we have need of every day. And since we need them every day, we also have daily opportunities to practice them.

St. Francis also suggests that we consider which virtues are most required for our state of life. "Different virtues are incumbent upon a bishop, a prince, or a soldier—the wife has her duties and the widow hers, and although all should practice every virtue, still each should seek chiefly to advance in those peculiarly required by the state of life to which God has called them." Both monks and married couples must practice the virtue of obedience, but in different ways. Those who teach small children must excel in patience. The rich are called to be especially generous with their wealth.

Finally, St. Francis cautions us to strive after the most excellent virtues and not the most popular, recognizing that the virtues that are "highly esteemed and preferred by ordinary men" are not necessarily the worthiest. In our day, for example, having a good diet and a regular exercise routine are seen as praiseworthy virtues—and, of course, they are—so everyone will applaud you for pursuing them.

---

[73] Quotations in this chapter are taken from part 3, chapter 1.

But they are less important to our spiritual life than the virtues of humility and patience, which often go unnoticed by others.

In discerning which virtues to focus on, we should also consider our natural temperaments. Although we should practice all the virtues, we are not all called to practice each one to the same degree. You can see this clearly in the lives of the saints in whom a special virtue often shines forth. St. Francis of Assisi was devoted to poverty. St. Teresa of Ávila was devoted to prayer. St. Damien of Molokai spent himself in service to lepers, and St. John Bosco was called to educate youth. The special virtues God calls us to practice in our lives provide the context for us to flourish in all the virtues. For example, by serving the poor of Calcutta, Mother Teresa grew not only in charity but also in fortitude, temperance, faith, humility, and so forth.

The vices we possess should also be taken into account. If we struggle with a particular vice, we need to work diligently to grow in its opposite virtue. This is how we strengthen our defenses against temptation. If I have no inclination to greed, I don't need to focus my efforts on growing in generosity. But if my weakness is pride, I ought to be very intentional about growing in humility. If I suffer from lust, I must devote myself to chastity. Vice is habitual sin, so to conquer vice, we must form opposing habits of goodness. That's the *Catechism* definition of virtue: "an habitual and firm disposition to do the good" (1803).

Remember always: the goal of the devout life is not to *do good*. We cannot earn our way to Heaven. The goal is to *be good*, because God is good, and we are made in His image (the image of goodness). To be good is to be more authentically ourselves!

Before we begin the work of growing in virtue, we must recognize that we cannot succeed in this task on our own. We must rely at all stages on prayer and the grace afforded us in the sacraments.

But this doesn't mean that God does all the work for us. He expects (and rewards) our cooperation. As St. Augustine observes, "God created us without us: but he did not will to save us without us."[74] The *Catechism* teaches that "moral virtues are acquired by human effort" and dispose us "for communion with divine love" (1804). Growing in virtue—working to become a better human being and therefore a better image of God—is work; but it's the work of the Christian life.

---

[74]   St. Augustine, *Sermon 169*, quoted in CCC 1847.

## Questions for Reflection

1. Which two or three virtues do you have the opportunity to practice daily in your state in life?
2. Which one or two vices do you struggle with the most? What are their opposite virtues?
3. Which saints inspire you, and which virtues do they exemplify?

## Scripture for Meditation

[Wisdom] I loved and sought after from my youth... For she leads into the understanding of God, and chooses his works... If one loves righteousness, whose works are virtues, she teaches moderation and prudence, righteousness and fortitude, and nothing in life is more useful than these. (Wisd. 8:2, 4, 7)

2

# Patience

In discussing virtue, the *Catechism* focuses on the four natural virtues of temperance, prudence, justice, and fortitude and the three theological virtues of faith, hope, and charity. But if you ask the average person to name a virtue, the answer you are most likely to hear will be "patience."

"Patience is a virtue" is a truism that many of us, as children, heard our parents express when we complained about having to wait to open Christmas presents or to save up our allowance for that special purchase. The phrase comes from an ancient Latin maxim: *maxima enim, patientia virtus*, or "patience is the highest virtue." St. Paul would argue that the greatest virtue is love (see 1 Cor. 13:13), but he points out that "love is patient" (1 Cor. 13:4). To grow in love, therefore, we must cultivate the virtue of patience.

We usually think of patience as the willingness to wait graciously for a good that we desire—as, for example, a child waiting for a birthday gift or an engaged couple waiting for their wedding day to consummate their marriage. Patience is the virtue that allows us to persist in school to earn a diploma, to save money to take a special trip, or to stick with a diet to lose weight. Instant gratification is cheap and fleeting, but good things come to those who wait.

But there is another side to patience. In addition to waiting for something good, patience also allows us to endure something evil. Whether it's a natural evil, such as illness; a moral evil, such as persecution; or even a minor annoyance, such as the fact that your spouse never empties the dishwasher, patience helps us graciously bear suffering with charity.

Waiting for good and enduring evil can be thought of as two sides of the same coin. Wanting a good you don't have and enduring an evil you don't want both involve a degree of suffering. Suffering is a part of life, and the Christian life is no exception. While we maintain the firm hope of eternal joy and rest in Heaven, our life on earth consists of taking up our cross daily to follow Christ (Luke 9:23). St. Augustine points out that the strength of the Christian is "not only to do good works but also to endure evil."[75] Patience is the virtue that allows us to transform suffering into penance—something that draws us closer to God.

St. Francis de Sales writes, "The virtue of patience is that which secures us the greatest perfection," and "to attain perfection, we must endure our imperfection."[76] He echoes St. Paul's exhortation to work out our salvation with fear and trembling (Phil. 2:12) when he writes, "We too on our part must work out our salvation by sufferings and afflictions, bearing injuries, contradictions, and annoyances with the greatest calm and gentleness."[77]

Ironically, it is often the small annoyances that prove most challenging. Many are willing to endure great afflictions courageously but complain miserably about the minor daily nuisances God would have us bear. St. Francis observes that some are happy to suffer great afflictions if they bring great honor. He gives the example of a soldier who is wounded in battle and who finds his pain easier to endure because he knows others will see him as a

---

[75] St. Augustine, *Sermon 46*, quoted in the Office of Readings for the Twenty-Fifth Sunday in Ordinary Time.

[76] *Consoling Thoughts*, 28.

[77] Quotations in this chapter are taken from part 3, chapter 3.

hero. Christians can fall victim to the same temptation by feeling self-righteous when we suffer for our Faith. "Such persons," St. Francis writes, "are lovers, not of the trials, but of the honor that accompanies them." Instead, "we must bear the particular complaint which God sends us," whatever it may be, even if no one sees us bearing it.

To endure suffering with charity, we should strive to avoid complaining. Complaints often arise from a lack of humility. We complain because our egos are offended or because we don't receive the attention or affirmation we desire. Complaining about others easily devolves into gossip or calumny, which are serious sins. It is easy to see why Scripture so often warns against "grumbling" (see 1 Cor. 10:10; Phil. 2:14; James 5:9; 1 Pet. 4:9).

On the other hand, there can be justifiable reasons to complain. Sometimes a legitimate situation will need to be brought to someone's attention. There is also the therapeutic value of "blowing off steam." So instead of telling us never to complain, St. Francis de Sales offers advice on how to complain prudently.

His first suggestion is to "complain as little as possible of the wrongs which are done to you; for it is certain that ordinarily he who complains sins." But if we must make a complaint either to address an injustice or to calm our spirit, he says we must be prudent about whom we complain to. "Above all do not complain to such persons as are prone to wax indignant and to think evil." Such people, he says, will only provoke our troubled spirit further. "Instead of removing the thorn which is pricking you, they will drive it deeper into your foot." He advises that we complain instead to "such persons as are peaceable and love God."

In other words, we should complain to people who can calm us down instead of riling us up. Complaining to a peaceable person allows us to blow off steam, but complaining to someone who loves conflict will only inflame our passions. I would add to the saint's advice that if we are complaining about a wrong that needs addressing, we should take care to make our complaint dispassionately to those who are in a position to address the matter. In all cases, we should seek to avoid gossip and not complain to those who are prone to gossip.

St. Francis de Sales also warns not to refrain from complaint for the wrong reasons. He writes, "There are some who when they are sick, afflicted, or aggrieved, avoid complaining ... [but] desire greatly that others should lament over them, and employ various means to induce them to do so, and would fain be counted patient and brave as well as afflicted." In other words, they intentionally avoid complaining about their suffering so that others will notice them not complaining. St. Francis says, "Theirs is a false patience, which in truth is only a refined ambition and vanity." This is a form of pride.

Patience doesn't require us always to suffer in silence but simply to be humble and honest, not making our problems out to be smaller or greater than they are. "A truly patient man neither complains himself nor wishes others to complain for him; he speaks honestly, simply, and truly of his trial without complaining, bemoaning, or exaggeration; and if he is pitied he receives pity with patience likewise." By neither hiding nor calling undue attention to your difficulty, St. Francis says, you will "rest calmly in truth and patience."

As parting wisdom, St. Francis de Sales references John 16:21: "When a woman is in labor, she has pain, because her hour has come; but when she is delivered of the child, she no longer remembers the anguish, for joy that a child is born into the world." As Christians, we have conceived Christ in our souls and are now laboring to deliver Him. This involves pain in the here and now, but it leads to unending joy on that great day when Christ will be fully formed in our hearts. In the meantime, St. Francis says, "offer to Christ our Lord all your pains, your suffering, and your languor, and beseech him to unite them to those he bore for you."

That this is easier said than done, the saints know very well. Our struggle with impatience is an invitation for us to be patient with ourselves. Here St. Francis offers the sage and practical advice: "Have courage, and take a long breath."[78]

---

[78] *Consoling Thoughts*, 33.

## Questions for reflection

1. What are some good things that you have had to wait for? Would you value them as much if you hadn't had to wait for them?
2. What are some hardships you have been called to endure? What made them easier or more difficult to endure?
3. How would you describe the difference between expressing a legitimate concern or grievance and the type of complaining St. Francis cautions us to avoid?

## Scripture for Meditation

Be still before the Lord and wait in patience....
Calm your anger and forget your rage;
do not fret, it only leads to evil.
For those who do evil shall perish;
the patient shall inherit the land.
(Ps. 37:7, 8–9)[79]

Love is patient. (1 Cor. 13:4)

God is love. (1 John 4:8)

---

[79] Grail Psalms (1963), as quoted in *The Liturgy of the Hours*.

# 3

# Humility

I once had a pastor who never tired of telling his congregation that the three most important virtues are "humility, humility, and humility." St. Francis de Sales would agree. He asserts that "all the saints, and especially the King of Saints and His Mother, ever honored and cherished this virtue above all others" (3, 4). The *Catechism*, after defining *prayer* as the "raising of one's mind and heart to God" goes on to say that "humility is the foundation of prayer" (2559). In other words, it is impossible to approach God without humility.

Humility is often misunderstood. Some think that humility means thinking poorly of ourselves. This is false. Humility means thinking *rightly* of ourselves. It is achieved not by thinking less of ourselves but by thinking of ourselves less. Humility is all about recognizing the truth about ourselves and who we are before God. The word comes from the Latin *humus*, which means "dirt" or "earth." It reminds us of our origins. "The LORD God formed the man out of the dust of the ground and blew into his nostrils the breath of life" (Gen. 2:7). It also reminds us of our end. "You are dust, and to dust you shall return" (Gen. 3:19).

This is why the publican's prayer is more effective than the Pharisee's. In Luke's Gospel we read that "the Pharisee spoke this prayer to himself, 'O God, I thank you that I am not like the rest of humanity—greedy, dishonest, adulterous—or even like this tax collector. I fast twice a week, and I pay tithes on my whole income'" (Luke 18:11-12). Good for him. Those are all good things. But the Pharisee is so confident in his own goodness that he doesn't recognize his need for God. That's why he speaks his prayer "to himself."

By contrast, the publican beats his breast and prays, "O God, be merciful to me a sinner" (Luke 18:13). His prayer is effective because it is true. It recognizes correctly who he is (a sinner), whom he petitions (God), and what he needs (mercy). This is the essence of humility; recognizing that we are creatures, that God is the Creator, and that everything we have comes from Him. "What do you possess that you have not received? But if you have received it, why are you boasting?" (1 Cor. 4:7).

St. Francis de Sales says, "Before we can receive the grace of God into our hearts, they must be thoroughly empty of all self-glory" (3, 4). When we are full of ourselves, there is no room for God. This is why the ultimate sin is pride. Pride takes our God-given capacity to love others and inverts it, turning it inward, so that it becomes a disordered self-love. The prideful person cannot serve God because he serves only himself. Satan fell because of pride. This makes humility (pride's opposite) a powerful weapon against the devil, because humility is repulsive to him.

It is said that Satan fears the name of Mary even more than the name of Jesus. This is because it's less of a blow to Satan's pride to be defeated by the great Son of God than to be defeated by His Mother, a humble woman. Mary is the model of humility. Because she was God's lowly handmaid, her soul magnified His greatness, and to this day, all generations call her blessed (see Luke 1:46-48).

Humility is a necessary aspect of the devout life, but it can be difficult to gauge our growth in this virtue because humility isn't boastful, even of itself. Only a prideful person says, "I am so humble!" St. Francis characterizes humility almost as being shy when he writes, "True humility does not affect to be humble, and makes few lowly speeches, for she not only desires to hide other virtues, but, above all, to hide herself" (3. 5). (You can see how humility and modesty are related). We must beware of the false humility that leads us to boast of how humble we are. This is just another manifestation of pride.

The humble person says neither "Look at how good I am" nor "Look at how bad I am" because both amount to saying, "Look at me." The humble person instead says, "Look at God." Humility means accepting both what is good and what is bad about yourself without excuse, exaggeration, or boasting, giving thanks to God for your strengths and asking God's mercy for your weakness.

It is not against humility to honestly acknowledge the gifts we have received from God and to use those gifts in His service. In fact, part of being a Christian disciple is identifying, cultivating, and putting to use the gifts God gives us. "As each one has received a gift, use it to serve one another as good stewards of God's varied grace" (1 Pet. 4:10). St. Francis points out that although humility often conceals her gifts, she is always ready to produce them when charity requires it (3, 5). As long as we remember that our strength comes from God, we glorify God and not ourselves when we use our gifts well.

St. Paul spoke of his gifts as treasure held in earthen vessels, "that the surpassing power may be of God and not from us" (2 Cor. 4:7), and he boasted of his weakness "that the power of Christ may dwell with me ... for when I am weak, then I am strong" (2 Cor. 12:9-10). St. Francis de Sales writes, "For myself, I would neither boast of what I do know, nor pretend to be more ignorant than I am" (3, 5).

Nor does humility demand that we eschew worldly honors, if those honors are honestly earned and accepted without pride.

"Worldly honors are acceptable to him who receives them indifferently without resting in them or seeking them eagerly," St. Francis asserts, "but they become very dangerous and hurtful to him who clings to and takes delight in them" (3, 4). The humble person bears honors and rank lightly, neither seeking them nor thinking himself superior because of them.

And although humility does not preclude our having a good reputation, the humble person should not place unwarranted value on the opinion of others. St. Francis advises that a good reputation is important, but not as important as a good life. A good reputation should be a signpost pointing to where virtue resides. If we lack virtue, having a good name is meaningless. It's like a sign pointing nowhere. St. Francis cautions us instead to "keep our eyes fixed on our Crucified Saviour, and go on in his service in simple-hearted confidence, with discretion and prudence: He will watch over our reputation" (3, 4).

In the Litany of Humility composed by Cardinal Rafael Merry del Val, we do not ask not to be honored or praised but to be free from the *desire* for honor and praise. What God wants from us most is a humble heart (see Ps. 51:19) open to receiving His mercy, because a humble heart is a heart like God's.

## Questions for Reflection

1. What strengths do you think you possess? Do you use those strengths to glorify God or yourself?
2. What is the difference between "thinking less of yourself" and "thinking of yourself less?"
3. Society today places a great importance on the notion of self-esteem and the accolades that come from working hard. Do you think that either of those things hampers the pursuit of humility?

## Scripture for Meditation

Have among yourselves the same attitude that is also
    yours in Christ Jesus,
Who, though he was in the form of God,
did not regard equality with God something to be
    grasped.
Rather, he emptied himself,
taking the form of a slave,
coming in human likeness;
and found human in appearance,
he humbled himself,
becoming obedient to death,
even death on a cross. (Phil. 2:5–8)

## LITANY OF HUMILITY
### Rafael Cardinal Merry del Val (1865–1930)

*O Jesus! meek and humble of heart,* hear me.
*From the desire of being esteemed,* deliver me, Jesus.
*From the desire of being loved* …
*From the desire of being extolled* …

*From the desire of being honored ...*
*From the desire of being praised ...*
*From the desire of being preferred to others ...*
*From the desire of being consulted ...*
*From the desire of being approved ...*
*From the fear of being humiliated ...*
*From the fear of being despised ...*
*From the fear of suffering rebukes ...*
*From the fear of being calumniated ...*
*From the fear of being forgotten ...*
*From the fear of being ridiculed ...*
*From the fear of being wronged ...*
*From the fear of being suspected ...*

*That others may be loved more than I,*
    Jesus, grant me the grace to desire it.
*That others may be esteemed more than I ...*
*That, in the opinion of the world, others may increase*
    *and I may decrease ...*
*That others may be chosen and I set aside ...*
*That others may be praised and I unnoticed ...*
*That others may be preferred to me in everything ...*
*That others may become holier than I,*
*provided that I may become as holy as I should ...*
*Amen.*

4

# Gentleness

"Humility perfects us in regards to God, and gentleness in regard to our neighbor," writes St. Francis de Sales (3, 8).[80] Just as we should strive to be humble before God, we should cultivate a gentle disposition toward our fellow human beings. Gentleness is one of the fruits of the Holy Spirit, along with kindness and self-control (Gal. 5:22-23). The virtue of gentleness is equated with meekness, and our Lord teaches that "the meek shall inherit the land" (Matt. 5:5).

But what does it mean to be meek and gentle? It does not mean being a doormat or a pushover, and it certainly doesn't mean shying away from standing up for what is right and true. Meekness is not weakness. Gentleness is not cowardice. Gentleness is an aspect of charity. In fact, St. Francis calls it "the flower of charity" (3, 8). Charity calls us to regard others as "other selves" and to treat them as we would wish to be treated (Matt. 7:12). This calls for us to be compassionate and forgiving toward one another.

Gentleness is the opposite of wrath, or anger (one of the seven deadly sins). Anger can serve as a powerful obstacle to charity and a breeding ground for sin. In His teaching on the law, Jesus says, "You have heard that it was said to your ancestors, 'You shall not kill; and whoever kills will be liable to judgment.' But I say to you whoever is angry with his brother will be liable to judgment"

---

[80]  Ross translation.

(Matt. 5:21–22). Jesus gets to the heart of the matter. He is not equating anger with murder but is recognizing that it is the disordered passions of our hearts that give rise to sin. If we want to uproot sin from our lives, we have to look to the source. This is why St. Francis de Sales says, "I exhort you earnestly never to give way to anger, and never, under any pretext whatever, let it effect an entrance into your heart" (3, 8).

But isn't there such a thing as righteous anger? Wasn't Jesus Himself angry when He drove the money changers out of the temple and turned over their tables (John 2:13–16)? Is it not appropriate to feel anger when confronted with injustice? St. Francis acknowledges this, saying, "Undoubtedly, we must oppose what is wrong, and steadfastly check the vices of those under our care, but we must do so quietly and gently." But he also wisely observes that "no angry man ever thinks his anger unjust" (3, 8). Our actions should be motivated by justice and charity, not anger—whether we think our anger is justified or not.

What should you do when you experience anger? After all, you cannot control what emotions you feel nor how certain situations may affect you. Some people are naturally more hot-tempered than others. The fact that someone's anger is more quickly aroused by injustice does not mean that he is righteous—any more than an even-tempered person's calm means that he is uncaring. What is important is not how you feel about a situation but how you respond to it. Anger is dangerous because it is a powerful emotion that can lead you to respond in ways you otherwise wouldn't if you were calm. When you experience anger, you should be careful not to nurse it or allow it to fester, breeding bitterness and resentment. "As soon as you feel the slightest resentment," St. Francis instructs, "gather together your powers, not hastily or impetuously but gently and seriously" (3, 8), and ask God to help calm your anger.

Reflect, dispassionately, on why you are angry and at whom your anger is directed. Is your anger warranted by the circumstances? Are you irritated simply because someone offended your sensibilities? This is a symptom of pride. Are you upset over an injustice that you are in no position to remedy? This can also be a manifestation of pride, if you feel it is your duty to fix every problem. For many, watching the evening news can be a near occasion of sin! In this case, it is good to remember the advice of Br. Lawrence who, when he heard of injustices in the world, prayed that God would remedy them in His own time and way and did not allow his soul to be distressed by them.[81]

But what of the injustices we are in a position to do something about? We are called to "correct the vices of those under our care," as St. Francis points out. Who is under our care? Parents are called to correct their children, teachers their pupils, priests their parishioners, and so forth. If we're upset over a fault committed by one in our care, we should correct that person—but that correction must be motivated by charity and not anger. If a parent finds herself becoming frustrated with an unruly child, it is never wise for her to punish the child when she is angry. Much better for her to delay punishment until her emotions have calmed, so she can be sure her actions are motivated by concern for the good of her child and not her own passions.

And let's not forget, chief among those entrusted to our care is our own soul! St. Francis asserts that we must be gentle when correcting ourselves above all. We should never grow irritable with our imperfections. This stems from pride, "which is displeased at finding we are not perfect." Of course we are not perfect. We require correction and repentance. But "we correct ourselves more

---

[81] *The Practice of the Presence of God*, first conversation.

effectually," St. Francis writes, "by a quiet persevering repentance than by an irritated, hasty, passionate repentance" (3, 9). Instead of berating ourselves, we should encourage ourselves, as we would encourage anyone else who was under our care and needed our support.

This is especially important for us to remember as we strive to grow in the spiritual life. To grow in holiness and devotion is to cooperate with God's grace, and this is something we learn to do little by little, in increments. It can be easy to grow frustrated with ourselves, especially as we become more aware of our own imperfections as we strive to grow in virtue. We should take heart that God is patient with us (see 2 Pet. 3:15), and so we must be patient with ourselves. It will be His grace that brings success to our works, as long as we don't give up.

St. Francis gives us the example of a small child walking with her father. With one hand she gathers fruits and flowers along the path, and the other hand always holds tight to her father's. As they walk, she looks up to him, to make sure he approves of what she is doing. "So whilst with one hand you collect and use the good things of this world," St. Francis writes, "always with the other keep hold of your Heavenly Father, frequently turning to Him, in order to learn whether He approves your occupations and proceedings" (3, 10).

## Questions for Reflection

1. Do you experience anger frequently or rarely? What are the primary sources of anger in your life?
2. Beside your own soul, who else is in your care? What family and friends are you called to be supportive of? Do you find it difficult or easy to correct them?
3. St. Francis points out that no angry person thinks his anger unjust. How can you discern the difference between just and unjust anger? How does this affect how you respond to your anger?

## Scripture for Meditation

Be angry, but do not sin; do not let the sun set on your anger, and do not leave room for the devil.... All bitterness, fury, anger, shouting, and reviling must be removed from you, along with all malice. [And] be kind to one another, compassionate, forgiving one another as God has forgiven you in Christ. (Eph. 4:26-27, 31-32)

# 5

# Obedience

When Jesus entered the town of Capernaum, he was met by a Roman centurion whose servant was homebound, paralyzed and in pain. The centurion knew Jesus to be a healer, and so came pleading on his servant's behalf. Jesus said to the man, "I will come and cure him," but the centurion protested: "Lord, I am not worthy to have you enter under my roof; only say the word and my servant will be healed. For I, too, am a person subject to authority, with soldiers subject to me" (Matt. 8:5–9).

With these words, the centurion expressed his faith in Jesus' authority over creation. He knew that sickness and even death itself would obey Jesus' word. Yet Jesus Himself practiced the virtue of obedience. He was obedient to the will of the Father (Phil. 2:8) as well as to His earthly parents (Luke 2:51).

St. Francis de Sales writes that the three great means of obtaining charity are obedience, chastity, and poverty. "Obedience," he writes, "consecrates our heart, chastity our body, and poverty our worldly means to the love and service of God." Practicing obedience says to God, "My will is Yours." Practicing chastity says, "My body is Yours." And practicing poverty says, "My possessions are Yours." These three virtues together say to God, "All that I am and have are Yours." St. Francis calls these virtues the "three branches of the spiritual cross," and they are founded upon the fourth, which is humility (3, 11). St. Francis rightly compares these virtues to the Cross because each in its own way requires us to sacrifice our ego on the altar of devotion.

Obedience, chastity, and poverty are the three vows tradition-ally taken by those entering religious orders. If we are not monks, we may be tempted to think they have nothing to do with us. But all are called to holiness, as the Second Vatican Council asserts, so it follows that everyone is called to practice these foundational virtues according to their state in life. "We are all bound to practice these three virtues," St. Francis reminds us, "although not all to practice them in the same way" (3, 11).

St. Francis recognizes two types of obedience: imperative and voluntary. Imperative obedience is obedience to those who hold legitimate authority over us. Everyone is subject to some author-ity. Christians are subject to ecclesial authority, including their pastor, their bishop, and the Holy Father. Those who belong to religious orders are subject to their superiors. Married people are subject to their spouses ("Be subordinate to one another, out of reverence for Christ" [Eph. 5:21]). Children are subject to their parents ("Children, obey your parents [in the Lord], for this is right" [Eph. 6:1]). Students are subject to their teachers, employees to their employers, soldiers to their commanding officers, and so forth. Everyone is subject to God above all.

The thought of submitting to authority chafes against the mod-ern American attitude that places such high value on independence and autonomy. Obedience comes with some difficulty for those of us taught to question authority figures from our youth. But, as the *Catechism* reminds us, well-ordered human society relies upon some people being in positions of authority over others. "Every human community needs an authority to govern it" (1898). This is true of communities as large as nations or as small as families. Without authority to give order to society, there is chaos.

But no human being has absolute authority over another. This is because all human authority is, so to speak, borrowed. Ultimate authority belongs solely to the ultimate Author. "There is no authority except from God," St. Paul proclaims, "and those that exist [i.e., human authorities] have been established by God" (Rom. 13:1). Recognizing that all authority comes from God puts limits on human authority. St. Maximilian Kolbe, the Franciscan priest and missionary who gave his life in exchange for that of a family man in the Auschwitz death camp, wrote of the virtue of obedience in a letter:

> God, who is all-knowing and all-wise, knows best what we should do to increase his glory. Through his representatives on earth he continually reveals his will to us; thus it is obedience and obedience alone that is the sure sign to us of the divine will. A superior may, it is true, make a mistake; but it is impossible for us to be mistaken in obeying a superior's command. The only exception to this rule is the case of a superior commanding something that in even the slightest way would contravene God's law. Such a superior would not be conveying God's will.[82]

So, if a soldier is given an order by his commanding officer that violates the moral law, he is not bound to obey it. Instead, he must obey the higher authority of God. Likewise if a human government establishes a law that is unjust, the moral tradition of the Church teaches us that it is no true law at all and therefore should not be obeyed. But when it comes to legitimate direction given by those whom God has seen fit to grant authority over us, our willing obedience is a reflection of our obedience to God.

St. Francis de Sales says we are to obey our superiors in regard to the particular authority they have over us. Children should

---

[82] From the letters of Maximilian Kolbe, quoted in *The Liturgy of the Hours*, Office of Readings, for August 14.

obey their teachers in the classroom and regarding their studies, but teachers have no authority over their students' home life. Your boss can tell you what to do on the job regarding your work responsibilities, but he cannot dictate your domestic affairs. We should obey the laws of the Church regarding faith and morality and should obey the laws of our government in secular matters. Each of us should be aware of what specific authorities our state in life makes us subject to and the specific aspects of our life that are subject to them.

In addition to the imperative obedience we each owe to the authorities just mentioned, St. Francis writes of the voluntary obedience we owe to authorities to whom we have willingly and freely subjected ourselves, such as our confessors or spiritual directors. We do not choose our pastors, bishops, or parents, but we are free to choose a spiritual director or a confessor, and voluntarily placing ourselves under his authority in our spiritual life helps us to foster the virtue of obedience and advance in holiness and devotion.

In the same letter as the passage just quoted, St. Maximilian Kolbe writes:

Obedience is the one and only way of wisdom and prudence for us to offer glory to God. If there were another, Christ would certainly have shown it to us by word and example. Scripture, however, summed up his entire life at Nazareth in the word: *He was subject to them*; Scripture set obedience as the theme of the rest of his life, repeatedly declaring that he came into the world to do his Father's will.[83]

In keeping with the example of Christ, St. Francis de Sales instructs us to be obedient both in simple, easy things and in

---

[83]    Ibid.

difficult matters. Our obedience should be given promptly and cheerfully, without grumbling or complaining, and "above all," the saint writes, "in a loving spirit for the love of Him who for our sakes became obedient even unto the death of the Cross" (3, 11).

It is in obedience that we are to "work out" our salvation "with fear and trembling" (Phil. 2:12). Obedience sanctifies us because it makes us Christlike. By practicing obedience, we imitate our Savior, who, though possessing all authority as God, "did not regard equality with God something to be grasped" (Phil. 2:6) but humbled Himself to become one of us, taking on human nature, being obedient not only to God the Father, but to Mary and Joseph and even to Pontius Pilate, even to the point of death, and thereby was exalted over all.

"Let us love our loving Father with all our hearts," St. Maximilian Kolbe implores us. "Let our obedience increase that love, above all when it requires us to surrender our own will. Jesus Christ crucified is our sublime guide toward growth in God's love."[84]

---

[84] Ibid.

## Questions for Reflection

1. To which authorities do you owe obedience in your state in life? Over which aspects of your life do they have authority? Do you offer obedience to them willingly or grudgingly?
2. Are you in positions of authority over others? If so, how does your obedience to others affect the way you exercise authority over those in your care?
3. Obedience to those in authority over us is a way of exercising obedience to God. How might this understanding affect how you relate to authority figures you may struggle to obey?

## Scripture for Meditation

Though he was in the form of God, [Jesus] did not regard equality with God something to be grasped. Rather, he emptied himself, taking the form of a slave, coming in human likeness; and found human in appearance, he humbled himself, becoming obedient to death, even death on a cross. Because of this, God greatly exalted him and bestowed on him the name that is above every name, that at the name of Jesus every knee should bend, of those in heaven and on earth and under the earth, and every tongue confess that Jesus Christ is Lord, to the glory of God the Father. (Phil. 2:6–11)

# 6

# Chastity

A common misconception today equates chastity with celibacy. If this were the case, we might think of chastity as a special virtue for priests and monastics, consecrated virgins, or young people before marriage. But as St. Francis de Sales reminds us, "in truth everyone greatly needs this virtue," which he calls, "the lily of the virtues" (3, 12).

This is because chastity is not merely the absence of sexual activity; as it is defined in the *Catechism*, "Chastity means the successful integration of sexuality within the person and thus the inner unity of man in his bodily and spiritual being" (2337). Chastity is about integrity. When the *Catechism* speaks of "sexuality within the person," it references the fact that our sex is a part of our being and should therefore be properly integrated into all of our relationships, not only with others but also with God and with ourselves.

"God created mankind in his image; in the image of God he created them; male and female he created them" (Gen. 1:27). There is something in our maleness and femaleness that reflects the image of God in us, and if we disrespect our sexual nature through sin and abuse, that image of God becomes marred. If we misunderstand the nature and purpose of our sexuality, we misunderstand something important about how God made us. This is true of married, single, and celibate people.

I make a distinction between those who are single and those who have taken vows of celibacy. The former are simply unmarried but may become married, and if that is their hope, they should be preparing themselves even as single people to be good spouses; whereas those living under vows of celibacy have no intention of ever being married. Thus, the practice of chastity will look different in the lives of the monk, the married couple, the widow or widower, the adolescent, and the young adult in the dating world. But all are called to chastity, meaning all are called to integrate their sexuality authentically into their state in life.

The moral teachings of the Church invite us to consider the purpose of our actions. The Church has long recognized two purposes of the sexual act. The first is basic and biological: reproduction. This is a very high and noble purpose because this is how new human beings are created, and the Church considers human beings to be a very great good indeed. Human beings are made in the image of God, and every act of human reproduction is the work not only of the father and mother, who help to create the body of their child, but of God, who directly creates the soul.

But the Church understands that sexuality "is not something simply biological, but concerns the innermost being of the human person as such," as Pope St. John Paul II put it in his apostolic exhortation on the family, *Familiaris Consortio.* Thus the Church also recognizes a second purpose of the sexual act, which is the union of the spouses. In *Familiaris Consortio,* the Holy Father clearly states that sex "is an integral part of the love by which a man and woman commit themselves totally to one another until death."[85]

These two ends of the sexual act, procreative and unitive, are related to each other so as to form a whole. Every child brought into the world deserves to be created through an act of love and

---

[85] Post-synodal apostolic exhortation *Familiaris Consortio* (November 11, 1981), no. 11.

born into a family in which both parents are committed to raising their children, who are the fruits of their love, until death do they part. The virtue of chastity is therefore not only for the good of the individual but for the family and indeed society as a whole. Any use of our sexual capacity that does violence to either the procreative or the unitive end is considered a grave sin. Every sexual sin identified by the Church (contraception, homosexual acts, sex outside of marriage, masturbation, etc.) is considered sinful because it seeks the pleasure of sex without respect to its full meaning.

The Church may seem to have a lot of "rules" about sex, which can give the impression that the Church believes sex to be some dangerous beast that needs to be tamed. Indeed, a cursory reading of St. Francis de Sales's chapters on chastity may give this impression. He writes, for example, of marriage as a "remedy against concupiscence ... but it is a very violent, and consequently a dangerous remedy, unless used with discretion" (3, 12). But he speaks of the need, even in marriage, to avoid carnal lust that would do violence to the love husband and wife ought to have for each other as persons. The virtue of chastity falls under the cardinal virtue of temperance. Sex is pleasurable and, like all pleasures, needs to be moderated in respect to its end.

In truth, the reason the Church has many "rules" about sex is not because she thinks sex is bad but because she considers sex to be something very good—holy, in fact! Consider this: the Church doesn't have any rules about bread, when and how you should eat it, how much you can consume, or how it is to be handled and stored. But the Church has very many rules about the Holy Eucharist. This is because the Eucharist is sacred, and ordinary bread is not. It matters more what we do with the Eucharist, and it matters more what we do with our bodies, for the same reason. Our bodies are sacred. We are not common bread.

Chastity is a particularly difficult virtue to put into practice in our age because the world has a very schizophrenic attitude toward sex. On the one hand, it holds sex up to be the greatest good. You can't possibly live a fulfilled life unless you fully "explore your sexuality" and enjoy all the sexual pleasure you want, all the time. You can't go to the movies, turn on the television or open a magazine without getting the message that sex is the be-all and end-all of human existence.

On the other hand, society treats sex as if it's utterly unimportant. Contraception, casual sex, the "hookup" culture, rampant divorce, the infestation of pornography in all our media—all send the signal that sex is devoid of meaning. Just have fun with it. Even the concepts of *male* and *female* have been robbed of meaning. Our minds may buy into that lie, but our bodies cannot. Our bodies know that sex has meaning and that we are not toys to be played with. That's why so many people are deeply, psychologically wounded today.

The Church's more balanced and realistic view of human sexuality is the remedy for this schizophrenia. Sex has meaning. Our bodies have meaning. Sex is a great good and therefore needs to be respected. But it's not the greatest good. Sex is a gift from God, and no gift is as great as its Giver. This is why the Church values both marriage and celibacy. Celibate vocations give witness to the world that our relationship with God is most important and indeed can be richly satisfying.

For those struggling with the virtue of chastity, St. Francis de Sales offers this advice. Associate with chaste and virtuous persons. "Iron sharpens iron" (Prov. 27:17), so we should spend time with those who exhibit the virtues we wish to attain. And we should "read and often think on sacred things" (3, 13). We are blessed in our time to have the body of work known as *Theology of the Body*, given to us by our Holy Father Pope St. John Paul the Great. I suggest making a study of this work by reading it or any of the many books that have been published relating to it on the popular level.

Finally, St. Francis implores us to "abide ever nigh to Jesus Christ crucified, spiritually in meditation, and actually in the Holy Communion. For ... if you rest your heart upon Our Lord, who is the true chaste and Immaculate Lamb, you will speedily find that your heart and soul will be purified from all stains and lusts" (3, 13).

## Questions for Reflection

1. How does chastity play a role in your current state in life? Has it always played this role? How might your state in life change in the future, and how would this affect the way you practice chastity?
2. Given society's prevalent views on sexuality, do you find chastity more difficult to practice than other virtues? In what ways?
3. It can be difficult to find people outside the Church today who value chastity. Have you been able to cultivate friendships with others who share the Church's views on chastity?

## Scripture for Meditation

Now the works of the flesh are obvious: immorality, impurity, licentiousness, idolatry, sorcery, hatreds, rivalry, jealousy, outbursts of fury, acts of selfishness, dissensions, factions, occasions of envy, drinking bouts, orgies, and the like. I warn you, as I warned you before, that those who do such things will not inherit the kingdom of God. In contrast, the fruit of the Spirit is love, joy, peace, patience, kindness, generosity, faithfulness, gentleness, self-control. Against such there is no law. Now those who belong to Christ [Jesus] have crucified their flesh with its passions and desires. If we live in the Spirit, let us also follow the Spirit. (Gal. 5:19–25)

# 7

# Poverty

St. Francis de Sales discusses poverty from two perspectives in his *Introduction*: first, for those who are materially wealthy, and secondly, for those who are materially poor. Those who are materially wealthy may still practice the virtue of poverty by becoming poor in spirit, and St. Francis provides examples of saintly figures who have done so, such as St. Louis of France and St. Elizabeth of Hungary. Both of these royal saints lived simply despite their great wealth and used their earthly treasures in the service of the poor. But let's not pretend that it is easy.

Whenever Our Lord speaks of material riches, it is with a warning. "Amen, I say to you, it will be hard for one who is rich to enter the kingdom of heaven.... It is easier for a camel to pass through the eye of a needle than for one who is rich to enter the kingdom of God" (Matt. 19:23–24). Jesus says this after His encounter with a rich young man who sought Him out to ask an important question—the most important question: "What must I do to gain eternal life?" This man is asking the right question, and he is asking the right Person. He has actively sought out Jesus. Furthermore, we are told that he has followed the commandments his entire life (Luke 18:21). This young man is on the right path. Jesus tells him he lacks only one thing. Jesus says he must give his wealth to the poor and follow Him. We are told that the man "went away sad, for he had many possessions" (Matt. 19:22). It is the saddest verse in Scripture.

This man could have been an apostle and a saint! Instead, we don't even know his name.

By contrast, Jesus speaks of poverty as a blessing. "Blessed are you who are poor, for the kingdom of God is yours" (Luke 6:20). In Matthew's Gospel he adds the words, "Blessed are the poor *in spirit*" (Matt. 5:3). Spiritual poverty is more essential than material poverty, but the former is more difficult to attain without the latter.

St. Francis first addresses his advice on spiritual poverty to those who have wealth. Most of us may not think of ourselves as very wealthy, but I think we need to recalibrate our thinking; especially those of us who live in First World countries. My family would not be considered wealthy in the world's eyes. In fact, when my wife and I were first married, we lived for many years below the poverty line (as established by government definitions). But we had a house. We had more than sufficient food and clothing. We had a refrigerator and a freezer to keep all that food in. We had two working vehicles. We had a television connected to a satellite dish that received signals from all over the planet. We had a computer and high-speed Internet service, bringing a world of information to our fingertips. We were nominally poor and qualified for government assistance, but we had luxuries beyond the dreams of kings and princes of past ages. Even those considered poor today may have more wealth than the rich young man possessed, and so they should pay heed to Christ's warning.

So do we all have to give away everything we own and run off into the wilderness naked like St. Francis of Assisi? Some are indeed called to embrace material poverty as a vocation, but not everyone. The key is not to allow our possessions to possess us. St. Francis de Sales writes, "He is rich in spirit whose heart is in his riches, and whose riches fill his heart. He is poor in spirit who has not riches in his heart, nor his heart in riches" (3, 14). In other words, we must be careful not to become attached to our wealth. What occupies our bank accounts should not occupy our hearts.

"There is a difference," St. Francis points out, "between possessing poison and being poisoned." Apothecaries (pharmacists) have poisons, but are not poisoned themselves, because the poisons are in their shops and not in their bodies. We can think of riches like this. Scripture says that it is the "love of money," not money itself, that is the root of all evils (1 Tim. 6:10). As long as you keep your riches in your purse and not in your heart, St. Francis says, then you are poor in spirit.

Still, it is difficult for us not to become possessed by our possessions, and the more possessions we own, the more difficult it is. To fit through the narrow gate into Heaven, we have to let go of everything we're holding on to here on earth. The rich are holding on to a lot. The trick is to hold it lightly.

We must remember that our possessions are not our own. Everything we have comes from God and belongs to God. We are only stewards, or caretakers, of the parts of creation entrusted to us. Are we using our wealth in ways that are pleasing to God? The patriarch Joseph stored up grain and used the surplus to feed the hungry during a famine (see Gen. 41:47-57). The rich man in Jesus' parable stored his surplus grain for himself and died before he could use it. He is called a fool (see Luke 12:16-21).

St. Gregory the Theologian says, "Let us not labor to heap up and hoard riches while others remain in need"; otherwise we are "holding on to what belongs to someone else."[86] St. John Chrysostom goes so far as to say, "Not to enable the poor to share in our

[86] Oration 14, quoted in the Office of Readings, First Monday of Lent.

goods is to steal from them and deprive them of life. The goods we possess are not ours, but theirs."[87]

So St. Francis advises the rich to use their wealth for the benefit of those in need. "Always dispose of a part of your means by giving freely alms to the poor.... Undoubtedly God will restore it to you in this world as well as in the next, for nothing brings such prosperity as almsgiving" (3, 14). Over and above giving to the poor, we should love the poor, "since we become like to that which we love." St. Francis advises us to be poor with the poor; "mingle with them in the church, the street, and elsewhere. Be poor in speech towards them, speaking with them as their friend, but let your hands be rich, imparting to them freely of your abundance" (3, 14).

To those who experience real material poverty, St. Francis has this to say: "Have patience, you are in good company. Our Lord, our Blessed Lady, the Apostles, and numberless saints, were poor" (3, 16).

He distinguishes between those who are poor by choice, such as professed religious, and those who are poor by circumstance. The latter, he says, live in "real poverty." People may esteem the former, but the latter are often despised and rejected by society. This makes their poverty the more difficult to bear, but the more potentially rewarding if it is accepted in love as the will of God. St. Francis writes:

Do not complain of your poverty. Do not be ashamed of being poor, or of seeking charitable alms; receive what is given you in humility and bear refusals with meekness. Remember how our Blessed Lady traveled into Egypt with her dear Son, and how much contempt, poverty, and sufferings they endured. If you do the like, you will be very rich in your poverty. (3, 16)

---

[87] *Hom. in Lazaro* 2, 5:PG 48,992; quoted in CCC 2446.

## Questions for Reflection

1. What material possessions are you attached to? What might you do to reduce those attachments?
2. Do you contribute a portion of your income to the poor? What ways might you support those in need beyond monetary donations?
3. Have you needed help from others? Did you accept it willingly or grudgingly? How does this experience impact your attitude toward helping others in need?

## Scripture for Meditation

"Lord, when did we see you hungry and feed you, or thirsty and give you drink? When did we see you a stranger and welcome you, or naked and clothe you?" ... "Amen, I say to you, whatever you did for one of these least brothers of mine, you did for me." (Matt. 25:37–38, 40)

8

# Friendship

In the previous chapter, we saw that St. Francis de Sales said that we become like what we love. If this is true (and it is), we ought to be careful about the friendships we form. Friendship is mutual love shared between people. We become like our friends, so we should choose our friends wisely. We should seek friends who will help us to grow in virtue, to become better people, and to advance in holiness. In the same vein, we should strive to be the kind of friends who can help our friends to do the same. "Iron is sharpened by iron; one person sharpens another" (Prov. 27:17).

St. Francis praises holy friendships, but because our friends have such an effect on us, he also calls friendship "the most dangerous of all love." In addition to mutual affection, Francis teaches that friendship requires communication (or an exchange), and the quality of the friendship will vary according to the quality of what is communicated between the friends. "If these are vain and false, then the friendship is vain and false; and the more excellent those qualities exchanged, the higher will the friendship be" (3, 17).

Frivolous friendships are based on frivolous things. Children in school might seek to become friends with other children because they are popular, are good-looking, or have the newest toys. These kinds of friendships are not lasting and naturally pass away as we grow in maturity. True, lasting friendships are based on virtue. "Have no friendship save with those who can interchange virtuous love with you," St. Francis advises, "since the more your friendship stands on the foundation of virtue, the more perfect it will be" (3, 19).

He points out that he is not speaking of those friendships to which "nature and duty" call us: our relatives, neighbors, and benefactors. We must be friends with these as much as we are able, despite the quality of their character. St. Francis is speaking of the special friendships that we intentionally form and cultivate. The friendships that we choose for ourselves should be based on virtue; as long as they are, they will be of mutual benefit to both parties.

In evaluating a friendship, we should ask, "Is this person helping me to become a better person?" Even if you enjoy someone's company and have mutual affection, friendship can be false if it leads you away from God. St. Francis warns that "worldly friendship confuses the judgment, and makes people imagine they do well whilst really they are in sin, and induces them to accept all their false excuses and pretexts as substantial reasons" (3, 20). Does this friend challenge you to be more virtuous or only affirm you in your vice? If the latter, then that person is no friend. "Trustworthy are the blows of a friend; dangerous, the kisses of an enemy" (Prov. 27:6). St. Francis points out, "Our friend becomes our enemy if he would cause us to sin" (3, 22).

As a college campus minister, I often preach about the importance of virtuous friendship at the beginning of the academic year. I encourage the freshmen students at Mass to look around them in the pews. "These are the students who care enough about their faith to seek out the church and come to Mass on their first Sunday on campus," I say. "Become friends with them." Experience has shown me that the students who form good friendships tend to do better in all aspects of their lives because of the support they enjoy from those who really care about their good.

None of this is to say that you should be friends only with saints. None of us are perfect in this world. We are pilgrims on a journey toward the perfection we hope to attain in Heaven. You want to choose companions who will help and not hinder you on that journey. But even the most virtuous of friends will have faults, and since we become like what we love, we should take care to imitate our friends' virtues and not their imperfections. St. Francis writes:

> When we esteem highly him whom we love ... we open our whole heart to the object of our friendship, and readily receive his inclinations and impressions, whether they be good or bad.... Unquestionably you should love him despite his imperfections; but neither love nor follow them, for friendship requires the communication of what is good, not of what is bad. (3, 22)

We all have enough faults of our own without adopting those of our friends! Rather, friendship obliges us "to strive mutually to overcome all such failings (3, 22)." If we want our friends to help us grow in virtue, we need to help them grow in virtue as well. We should be the kind of friends we want to have.

Friendships can be based on mutual love of all kinds of things. Friends can bond over their shared love of music, science, sports, or politics. But the highest friendships are based on the mutual love of God. These are the friends who will help you get to Heaven.

History is full of examples of saintly friendships we can emulate. St. Francis mentions the special friendships that existed between Our Lord and St. John, St. Mary Magdalene, and Lazarus, Martha, and Mary of Bethany. St. Peter was friends with St. Mark, as was St. Paul with St. Timothy. St. Francis dwells especially on the friendship shared between St. Gregory Nazianzen and St. Basil.

Both men were born in the year 330. Both lived for a time as hermits and later became bishops; Basil was bishop of Caesarea and Gregory of Constantinople. What made their friendship legendary, even among the saints, was their mutual love of God and firm commitment to holiness.

St. Gregory, who outlived his friend by a decade, wrote of their friendship in a sermon that is included in the Office of Readings on January 2, their (appropriately) shared feast day.

> When, in the course of time, we acknowledged our friendship and recognized that our ambition was a life of true wisdom, we became everything to each other: we shared the same lodging, the same table, the same desires, the same goal. Our love for each other grew daily warmer and deeper.... We seemed to be two bodies with a single spirit.... Our single object and ambition was virtue, and a life of hope in the blessings that are to come.... With this end in view we ordered our lives and all our actions. We followed the guidance of God's law and spurred each other on to virtue. If it is not too boastful to say, we found in each other a standard and rule for discerning right from wrong.[88]

Cultivating holy friendships on earth prepares us for the life of Heaven, where we will enjoy friendship not only with the saints but with God Himself. This is an astounding thing to consider, for friendship requires not only mutual love but a certain equality. It is difficult, if not impossible, for parents to be friends with their children, workers to be friends with their bosses, or soldiers to be friends with their commanding officers. Yet God, the Author of

---

[88] St. Gregory Nazianzen, *Oratio 14*, quoted in the Office of Readings for January 2.

Creation, the Alpha and the Omega, the Ancient of Days, calls us His friends. We are not equal with God, but that is no longer an obstacle, for God has made Himself equal to us in Christ Jesus.

Jesus tells us, "I no longer call you slaves, but friends" (John 15:15). He tells us that there is no greater love than to lay down one's life for a friend (John 15:13), and then he does just that for us. And he invites us into friendship with him, saying, "you are my friends if you keep my commands" (John 15:14). If we relate to Jesus as a friend, we will receive His commands not as dictates laid down by a tyrant but as the wise counsel of a friend who has our best interests at heart. We will say with the psalmist, "Lead me, Lord, in the path of your commandments," and "teach me your statutes...in your statutes I take delight" (Ps. 119:12, 16, 35).

Virtuous human friendship must be rooted in the friendship of God. There may be times when the friendship of God is the only friendship we know. If that is all we have, let us know that it is enough.

## Questions for Reflection

1. How do your relationships with your family members and neighbors (with whom you may be friendly) differ from your relationships with friends that you choose based on common interests?
2. Think of a particular friend. Is that person helping you become holier? Does he or she challenge you to become more virtuous or affirm you in your vices?
3. What does it mean for you to know God not only as your Master, Teacher, and Creator but also as your friend?

## Scripture for Meditation

Faithful friends are a sturdy shelter;
whoever finds one finds a treasure.
Faithful friends are beyond price,
no amount can balance their worth.
Faithful friends are like life-saving medicine;
those who fear God will find them.
Those who fear the Lord enjoy stable friendship,
for as they are, so will their neighbors be."
   (Sir. 6:14–17)

9

# Fasting

Growing in virtue requires an increase in spiritual discipline that is greatly aided by means of ascetic penances. Asceticism is the denial of some pleasure of the senses. Penance is a pious practice undertaken to help us repent, i.e., to turn away from sin and orient our hearts back to God. So an ascetic penance is any denial of sensual or bodily pleasure for the purpose of helping us grow closer to God and to remain firm in our faith. It helps build the virtue of temperance, which allows us to enjoy the good things of this world in moderation so they don't become our gods.

There are many forms of ascetic penance and self-denial, but the one with the longest track record of success is undoubtedly fasting. Fasting is penance that literally hits us in the gut. It was practiced by the Jewish people on the Day of Atonement, described in Leviticus as a time to express repentance for sins by prayer, fasting, and sacrifice. In the book of Tobit, the angel Raphael speaks of the importance of prayer, fasting, and giving alms to the poor (Tob. 12:8). Before Queen Esther approaches King Ahasuerus to beg mercy for her people, she asks the Jewish community to make a three-day fast for her intentions (Esther 4:16).

Our Lord Himself fasted for forty days in the desert before the start of His public ministry. In Matthew's Gospel, John's disciples asked Jesus, "Why do we and the Pharisees fast much, but your disciples do not fast?" (Matt. 9:14). Jesus responds, "Can the wedding guests mourn as long as the bridegroom is with them? The days will come when the bridegroom is taken away from them, and then they will fast" (Matt. 9:15). And indeed they did. The earliest post–New Testament documents, including the *Didache* and *The Shepherd of Hermas*, tell us that the early Christians continued to practice fasting as part of their religious observance.

St. Francis de Sales mentions several benefits of fasting—namely, "lifting up the mind, subduing the flesh, strengthening virtue, and earning an eternal recompense." He writes also that fasting helps us "keep the body and its appetites subject to the law of the spirit."[89] The aim of fasting is to discipline the body so that we are not subject to every passion or desire that comes our way; that we don't treat our stomach as our God (see Paul's warning in Philippians 3:19). By developing the discipline to say no even to legitimate pleasures, we learn to resist more easily the temptation of illegitimate pleasure. Fasting helps us to learn the lesson that "one does not live by bread alone, but by every word that comes forth from the mouth of God" (Matt. 4:4). For this reason, St. Francis says, "Satan is the more afraid of those who, he is aware, know how to fast."

Church discipline regarding fasting has changed over time. In our age, canon law establishes Ash Wednesday and Good Friday as the only two obligatory days of fasting for Catholics who are eighteen to fifty-nine,[90] though in their 1966 *Pastoral Statement on Penance and Abstinence*, the U.S. Bishops recommend "a self-imposed observance of fasting" on all weekdays of Lent.[91]

Fasting is understood to mean eating only one meal during the day. It is described by Pope St. Paul VI this way in his Apostolic

---

[89] Quotations in this chapter are taken from book 3, chapter 23.

[90] Can. 1251, 1252.

[91] United States Council of Catholic Bishops, *Pastoral Statement on Penance and Abstinence* (November 18, 1966), no. 14.

Constitution *Paenitemini*: "The law of fasting allows only one full meal a day, but does not prohibit taking some food in the morning and evening, observing—as far as quantity and quality are concerned—approved local custom."[92] This is the origin of the "two smaller meals that together do not equal one full meal" phrase that gets repeated so often during Lent; although technically true, however, the phrase gives the unfortunate impression that fasting still allows eating three times per day. This was not Pope Paul VI's intent. One meal per day is the norm for fasting, but if you need to take additional food, you may do so without being scrupulous about it. Since fasting is understood to mean limiting yourself to one meal, however, if that additional food equates to another meal, you are no longer fasting at that point. I should add that if you truly need that second meal, you are not bound by the law of fasting in any case. Fasting is about spiritual discipline, not harming the body, and the Church's fasting laws are quite minimal for this reason.

We should keep in mind that the times of fasting established by ecclesial law represent a minimum. If all we observe is the minimum required, we may avoid sin, but we miss out on opportunities for spiritual growth. St. Francis de Sales advises, "If you are able to fast, you will do well to observe some abstinence beyond what is enjoined by the Church." Even while encouraging the practice of fasting beyond the minimum required by law, St. Francis cautions moderation. "I disapprove of long and immoderate fasting, especially for the young," he writes, for "when young people are enfeebled by excessive fasting, they are easily led into self-indulgence and luxury." In other words, if we burn out on fasting, there is a

---

[92]  Pope Paul VI, apostolic constitution *Paenitemini* (February 17, 1966), III, 2.

danger of the pendulum swinging in the other direction, especially in those who lack maturity.

When fasting it is important to preserve bodily health. St. Francis notes that just as we cannot carry the body if it is too fat, it cannot carry us if it is too lean. Both "fasting and labor... exhaust the flesh," he writes. "If your labor is necessary or serviceable to the glory of God, I should select for you the discipline of labor in preference to that of fasting." Lest we think our sage guide has in mind only hard manual labor, he provides for us these examples. "One finds his labor in fasting, another in nursing the sick, visiting prisoners, hearing Confessions, preaching, comforting the afflicted, in prayer and similar exercises."

We should be modest in our fasting. St. Francis recalls Jesus' instructions to the seventy-two disciples He sent on mission without money bag, sack, or sandals: "Eat what is set before you" (Luke 10:8):

> I think that there is more profit in eating whatsoever food is offered you, whether it suits your taste or not, than in always choosing the worst. For although the latter practice appears more austere, the former is more submissive.... There is considerable mortification in entirely subduing all tastes and subjecting them wholly to circumstances."

Fasting teaches us to deny not only our bodies but our preferences and desires—even a desire for fasting! For example, we might decide to make Wednesdays and Fridays days of abstinence from meat (one of the recommended disciplines for those enrolled in the Brown Scapular of Mount Carmel). If we were then invited to a dinner on a Wednesday and our host served us steak, it would be a greater act of self-denial for us to eat the steak rather than to embarrass our host by making a fuss.

In deciding which forms of fasting or other ascetic penance may be beneficial for us to take on, we would do well to consult with our spiritual director and remember St. Francis's advice: "A continued, habitual temperance is far better than occasional, rigid abstinence alternating with great relaxation."

The purpose of Christian fasting is not only to discipline the body but to purify the heart; this is why the Church recommends that fasting be accompanied by prayer and charitable works. The prophet Isaiah reveals that the fasting of Israel was not heeded by God because "on your fast day you carry out your own pursuits, and drive all your laborers" (Isa. 58:3). The Lord says "[This is] the fast that I choose: releasing those bound unjustly ... setting free the oppressed ... sharing your bread with the hungry, bringing the afflicted and homeless into your house, clothing the naked when you see them.... Then you shall call, and the Lord will answer" (Isa. 58:3, 6-9).

## Questions for Reflection

1. What sort of Lenten fasts have you practiced? What spiritual gains, if any, have you made by those practices? Do you feel as if your fasting has been too lax or too severe?

2. Are there bodily or sensual pleasures other than food that you might deny yourself as ascetical penances? What benefits might you gain from doing so?

3. Have you ever considered fasting outside the Lenten season? What degree of fasting would be reasonable for you to take on throughout the year?

## Scripture for Meditation

When you fast, do not look gloomy like the hypocrites. They neglect their appearance, so that they may appear to others to be fasting. Amen, I say to you, they have received their reward. But when you fast, anoint your head and wash your face, so that you may not appear to others to be fasting, except to your Father who is hidden. And your Father who sees what is hidden will repay you. (Matt. 6:16–18)

# 10

# Modesty

Human beings are social creatures, and very few are called to be hermits. Most of us, therefore, spend a significant amount of our time interacting with others and should learn to do so virtuously so that the society we keep does not become an occasion of sin.

St. Francis encourages moderation in all our social interaction. Both to crave society and to shun it altogether he calls "blamable extremes" (3, 24). The terms *introvert* and *extrovert* did not exist in his day, but St. Francis often warns us not to allow our natural temperaments to become excuses for vice. Always shunning society indicates disdain for our neighbor, whom we are called to love, and always needing to be in the company of others indicates disdain for ourselves and our own company.

Being a natural introvert is not an excuse for being rude and standoffish. To refuse to engage in conversation, St. Francis says, indicates "a lack of confidence or some degree of contempt" for those we are with. On the other hand, "perpetual chatter and gossip, which gives no one else time or opportunity to speak, is trifling and vexatious." Being a natural extrovert is no excuse for being pushy or in one's face. We should learn to moderate our natural temperaments. "At all times," St. Francis writes, "let simplicity, candor, gentleness, and modesty prevail in conversation" (3, 24).

Note his use of the term *modesty*. Modesty and moderation go hand in hand. Both come from the Latin word *modus*, which means "measure." We are used to thinking of modesty today primarily in terms of clothing, but the *Catechism* calls modesty "an integral part of temperance" that "guides how one looks at others and behaves toward them in conformity with the dignity of persons and their solidarity" (2521). Modesty is more than a dress code. It is about conducting ourselves in society in a manner that respects our neighbor and ourselves.

In terms of dress, St. Francis commends cleanliness and propriety, which he observes, "depends upon various circumstances, such as time, age, rank, those with whom you associate; and it varies with different occasions" (3, 25). There are no hard-and-fast rules of modesty in fashion because fashion deals with social norms, which change over time and vary from place to place. St. Francis would have us be aware of and respect these norms as a means of respecting the sensibilities of those whom we are with. What is proper to wear to a football game is not proper to wear to a wedding. What we wear to a casual dinner with friends is not what we wear to a formal business dinner. What may be appropriate clothing for a fourteen-year-old is undignified on a forty-five-year-old.

We shouldn't seek to make a show of ourselves by the way we dress or the manner of our conduct. "Adhere as far as possible to modesty and simplicity," he writes, "which, doubtless, are the best ornaments of beauty, and the best atonement for its deficiency" (3, 25). St. Ephraim the Syrian speaks of the whole comportment of the person when he advises, "Let your body be quiet and cheerful, your greeting seemly and simple; your discourse without fault, your speech brief and savory; your words few and sound."[93]

In terms of our speech, St. Francis notes that we should also be modest in the way we speak of God. "If, then, you have a hearty love of God," he writes, "you will frequently speak of him

---

[93] St. Ephraim, *Homily on Admonition and Repentance*, 11.

with your family, your friends, and neighbors" (3, 26). Christians should not hesitate to speak of holy things, but we should do so naturally. Have you ever met a Christian who was pushy in his attempt to evangelize? Such Christians end up having the opposite effect, driving people away from the discussion of religion. On the other hand, there are Christians who avoid speaking of God in public altogether, either from an exaggerated sense of reverence or a hesitation about their own knowledge. Avoid both extremes. Let your talk of God be natural, as if you were speaking of one friend with another. "And let it be with reverence and devotion, not pompously or as it were preaching, but with the spirit of gentleness, charity, and humility" (3, 26).

Taking the Lord's name in vain is a clear violation of the Second Commandment (see Exod. 20:7), but what of using foul language? Vulgar words are not in themselves sinful and may even be appropriate on occasion. In Philippians 3:8, St. Paul uses a vulgar term for human excrement, *skubala* (often euphemistically translated as "refuse"), to describe the worth of what the world has to offer compared with what we stand to gain in Christ. But ordinary use of vulgar language can be immodest and show a lack of respect for those around us. "Beware of ever using any impure expressions," St. Francis cautions, "for even if you have no bad intention, those who hear you may receive them differently" (3, 27).

Moderating our speech, our dress, and our overall conduct out of respect for those we are with goes beyond the virtue of temperance. It also requires humility, to avoid drawing undue attention to ourselves. And it is a simple way to practice charity as we learn to consider how our engagement in society is received by those around us, whom we are called to love.

*Questions for Reflection*

1. Are you more introverted or extroverted? How might you temper your natural tendencies either to avoid or to seek out society?

2. How do you consider modesty in terms of your whole comportment of self, and not just as a matter of clothing? What does it mean to be modest in speech or action?

3. Do you find it easy and natural to talk about God without preaching or proselytizing? Do you show proper respect and reverence for the name of God and other holy subjects?

*Scripture for Meditation*

Your adornment should not be an external one: braiding the hair, wearing gold jewelry, or dressing in fine clothes, but rather the hidden character of the heart, expressed in the imperishable beauty of a gentle and calm disposition, which is precious in the sight of God. (1 Pet. 3:3–4)

11

# Speaking of Others

We discussed foul language in the last chapter as a form of immodesty in speech. Much more harmful than vulgarity are words of rash judgment, calumny, and detraction. These are named in the *Catechism* as offenses against truth, which means they are offenses against God, who is Truth.

> *Respect for the reputation* of persons forbids every attitude and word likely to cause them unjust injury (cf. CIC, can. 220). He becomes guilty of *rash judgment* who, even tacitly, assumes as true, without sufficient foundation, the moral fault of a neighbor; of *detraction* who, without objectively valid reason, discloses another's faults and failings to persons who did not know them (cf. Sir. 21:28); of *calumny* who, by remarks contrary to the truth, harms the reputation of others and gives occasion for false judgments concerning them. (2477)

The Gospel forbids us to judge our neighbor (see Matt. 7:1); therefore any judgment of our neighbor is a rash one. St. Francis de Sales gives three very good reasons to avoid rash judgment. The first is that God is our judge, so when we judge others, we "usurp the office of Our Lord." The second is that "the chief guilt of sin depends upon the intention and thought of the heart," which are hidden to us. The third is that "everyone has enough to do in judging himself, without presuming to judge his neighbor" (3,

28). You are not God. You are not your neighbor. You *are* you, and that's whom you need to admonish.

"It is the sign of an idle mind to take delight in examining the lives of others," St. Francis observes (3, 28). Those occupied in finding the faults of others usually neglect their own faults. In his preaching on repentance, St. Ephraim the Syrian instructs us to "search not out the faults of men" but "reprove your soul and yourself. Be the judge of your own sins."[94]

None of this means we should not call a sin a sin. Admonishing the sinner is a spiritual act of mercy. But when we admonish another's sins, it should be done prudently and privately, with charity and not malice, taking care to preserve the reputation of the person as much as possible. This can be difficult and delicate, but St. Francis offers this practical advice:

When you blame the vices of another, consider whether it is profitable or useful to those who hear to do so.... If you chance to be the leading person in society when such subjects are named, and your silence would give you the appearance of approving vice, then you should speak; if on the contrary you are an insignificant member of the company, do not assume the censorship. Above all, you must be exceedingly exact in what you say; your tongue when you speak of your neighbor is as a knife in the hand of the surgeon who is going to cut between the nerves and tendons. Your stroke must be accurate, and neither deeper nor slighter than what is needed; and whilst you blame sin, always spare the sinner as much as possible. (3, 29)

[94] St. Ephraim, *Homily on Admonition and Repentance*, 12.

Charity requires us to assume that our neighbor has good intentions unless it is truly proven otherwise. It is good to assume that any sin or offense is committed out of ignorance. As St. Francis rightly observes, we cannot know the heart or mind of another at the time the person committed an offense or whether he or she has since repented. Jesus gives us a model to follow in His prayer for those who nailed Him to the Cross: "Father, forgive them, they know not what they do" (Luke 23:34).

None of this means we should abandon common sense when it comes to untrustworthy people. St. Francis clarifies that "we are forbidden to judge, not to doubt." If you know someone to be a gossip, prudence dictates that you watch your words around that person and not fuel his or her flame. If you know someone to be a thief, don't leave your wallet or purse unattended in that person's presence. "Still," St. Francis cautions, "we should not indulge doubt or suspicion without great caution, and only insofar as these are based on reason and argument" (3, 28).

Detraction is the sin of broadcasting another's true faults. Calumny is the sin of broadcasting another's false faults. We easily avoid both simply by not speaking ill of others. Everyone has a right to a good reputation. We ruin our own reputation by sinful actions, and we can ruin others' by our sinful words. St. Francis implores us, therefore, "never to speak ill of anyone." Don't accuse others of faults they do not have, don't exaggerate the faults they do have, and don't deny the good qualities they possess, "for all these things grievously offend God" (3, 29).

The exceptions are those St. Francis calls "notorious and infamous sinners"—those whose egregious sins are matters of public knowledge and should be recognized as such for the good of society. Even then, we should speak of them with charity and compassion. We should not delight in their fall or feel self-righteous about it. We can condemn their actions without condemning the persons.

St. Francis gives one final warning that seems especially appropriate in today's political climate, in which "politics" consists chiefly in doing whatever you can to ruin the reputation of politicians on the opposing side. "Everyone thinks himself at liberty to judge and censure princes, and to decry whole nations according to his inclinations," he writes. "Do not indulge this failing: it is displeasing to God, and may involve you in numberless disputes" (3, 29). We can be especially quick to judge government authorities, dragging their name through the mud, readily believing every bad thing we hear about them, delighting in any misstep they make. We excuse this by telling ourselves that they are public figures and "it goes with the territory."

Detraction and calumny are still sins, whether we are talking about our elected officials or our next-door neighbors. We should be mindful of the fact that those in government authority have access to information we do not have, and shoulder responsibilities that we do not bear. They will be judged by God according to the decisions that they make, for better or for worse. The Church rightly teaches us to pray for those in authority that they act with wisdom and prudence.

## Questions for Reflection

1. Do you find it easier to assume the good intentions of others in online platforms or in person? How does this affect your discourse on social media?
2. In what situations might it be prudent and necessary to disclose another's faults? How would you prevent that from falling into gossip, calumny, or detraction?
3. How might we approach political discourse in a more charitable way in our society?

## Scripture for Meditation

The lips of the arrogant talk of what is not their
    concern,
but the discreet carefully weigh their words.
The mind of fools is in their mouths,
but the mouth of the wise is in their mind.
When the godless curse their adversary,
they really curse themselves.
Slanderers sully themselves,
and are hated by their neighbors. (Sir. 21:25–28)

# 12

# Leisure

"If you do all in the name of God, you will do all well," St. Francis de Sales writes, "whether you eat or whether you drink, whether you sleep or repose from labor, whether you are engaged in honorable or menial offices" (3, 35). God knows how many hairs are on our heads and has numbered all of our days; therefore there is no human activity that is unimportant to Him, even our leisurely pastimes.

We may think our leisure activities unimportant, but it is good and necessary to relax both our bodies and our minds from time to time. St. Francis points out that if an archer were to keep his bow always strung, the bow would lose its spring and wouldn't function as well when needed (3, 31). Our modern society places a heavy emphasis on work and productivity. Too many Americans keep their bow strung all the time, as it were, and fall victim to burnout. There is value and dignity in human labor. This is taught by the Magisterium of our Church, especially in the encyclicals *Rerum Novarum* (1891) and *Laborem Exercens* (1981), written a century apart by Pope Leo XIII and Pope St. John Paul II. It is also taught by Scripture: "If anyone [is] unwilling to work, neither should that one eat" (2 Thess. 3:10).

Yet Scripture and Tradition also teach that work (or at least the drudgery of work) is a consequence of the Fall. In the beginning, man's task was to "cultivate and care for" the garden (Gen. 2:15), which naturally involved some effort and attentiveness. But after man's rebellion, his work became burdensome. "Cursed is the ground because of you!" God told Adam. "In toil you shall eat its yield.... By the sweat of your brow you shall eat bread" (Gen. 3:17, 19). But we were not made for eternal toil, which is why God tempers our work with a sabbath. The third commandment is to "remember the sabbath day—keep it holy" (Exod. 20:8), recalling the seventh day of creation, when God rested, and anticipating the eternal rest of Heaven.

God's rest is not idleness. He looked at everything He had made and found it good (Gen. 1:31). Rest and leisure create space in our lives for contemplation. When Moses asked Pharaoh to give the people of Israel time off from their labor to worship God in the wilderness, Pharaoh responded by giving them more work to do. "Increase the work for the men, so that they attend to it and not to deceitful words" (Exod. 5:9). If he could keep them busy enough, Pharaoh surmised, they wouldn't have time to think about their God. Taking time for leisure keeps us from making a false god of our work. The trick is to avoid making a false god of our leisure. It was King David's idleness that led him to lust after Bathsheba (2 Sam. 11:1-4).

In our leisure activities, as in all things, St. Francis advises moderation and discretion. Just as we shouldn't work so much as to allow no time for leisure, we shouldn't relax so much that we neglect our necessary work. A healthy schedule finds a proper balance between work, prayer, study, and leisure.

It should go without saying that we should not engage in sinful pastimes. But things such as "air and exercise, cheerful games, music, field-sports, and the like," St. Francis writes, "are such innocent amusements that they only require to be used with ordinary discretion, which confines all things to their fitting time, place, and degree." Whatever our preferred pastimes may be, St. Francis cautions against spending too much time on them, attaching too much importance to them, or allowing ourselves to become too absorbed in them. Essentially, we must not value them beyond their true worth. "However allowable such things are," he says, "they become evils as soon as they absorb the heart" (3, 31).

We can see this in the way some foster a near religious devotion to sports. Although St. Francis says games that exercise the body and mind are praiseworthy, when parents allow children to neglect their religious obligations to attend soccer practice, their priorities have become misplaced. How many people couldn't name the Twelve Apostles but can easily name every player on their favorite team? How many think nothing of missing Mass on occasion but would never dream of missing a game?

Even praiseworthy pastimes can become dangers to our souls if we give them more importance than they are due. We can see this easily in some people's obsession with sports, but it's possible to develop an unhealthy obsession with any pastime or hobby, be it reading novels, gardening, playing games, listening to music, or anything else. If we give our pastimes so much time and attention that we neglect our necessary obligations, they have become unhealthy.

St. Francis de Sales warns especially against dice, cards, and games of chance (3, 32). As the *Catechism* instructs us, these games are not sinful in themselves, but "become morally unacceptable when they deprive someone of what is necessary to provide for his needs and those of others. The passion for gambling risks becoming an enslavement" (2413).

We do well to remember that even in our leisure we are called to love and serve God. So let our leisure be wholesome, healthy, and pleasing to Him.

*Questions for Reflection*

1. Do you find it difficult to set aside time for leisure, or do you feel the need to constantly be productive, whether at work or at home?

2. Are there leisure activities that you feel take up too much of your time or that you tend to prioritize beyond their importance?

3. During your times of leisure, do you set aside time for contemplation as God did during His rest on the seventh day?

*Scripture for Meditation*

Come to me, all you who labor and are burdened, and I will give you rest. (Matt. 11:28)

13

# Selfishness

The trajectory of the spiritual life of a Christian leads from self-centeredness to other-centeredness, as we learn to give ourselves in love to God and neighbor. The pride and arrogance of Satan are defeated by the humility and obedience of Christ.

All of the self-affirming mantras of pop psychology teach us that each of us is the center of our own universe, the pilot of our own destiny, and the judge and jury of our soul. "You do you." "Whatever floats your boat." "Follow your heart." As Frank Sinatra sang, "I did it my way." That could be the theme song of Hell.

Christianity manages to be self-affirming without being self-centered. It is self-affirming because it teaches you that you are made in God's image; that God loves you enough to have created you, that He loves you like a father (more perfectly and intensely than any human father could), and that He loves you enough to forgive any wrongdoing, even to give His life for you. But Christianity is not self-centered—it is God-centered. And God loves your neighbors as much as He loves you. Thus, we are taught to love God first, as the highest good, and to love our neighbors as ourselves, because our neighbors are just as worthy of love as we are. To do this well, we must overcome the selfishness that we have all struggled with since the Fall.

A characteristic of selfish thought is that we tend to judge others by a different standard from which we judge ourselves. St. Francis de Sales writes:

We accuse our neighbors in little things but excuse ourselves in great things. We seek to buy cheap and sell dear. We demand justice towards others, but towards ourselves mercy and indulgence.... We are ready to complain of our neighbor, but we would have no one complain of us.... We have one measure whereby to weigh all that appertains to ourselves as advantageously as possible, and another for our neighbor as disadvantageous as may be. (3, 36)

All of this he condemns as contrary to reason and justice.

Jesus illustrates this inclination in the parable of the unforgiving servant. A servant who owed a huge debt to his master was unable to pay it back, so he begged his master for mercy, and the master forgave his debt. But that same servant, upon encountering a fellow servant who owed him a much smaller amount, refused to treat his debtor with similar mercy, having him thrown into prison instead. Upon hearing this, the master summoned him back. "You wicked servant!" he said. "I forgave you your entire debt because you begged me to. Should you not have had pity on your fellow servant, as I had pity on you?" (Matt. 18:32-33). "The measure with which you measure will be measured out to you" (Matt. 7:2).

"Put yourself into your neighbor's place," St. Francis writes, "and him in yours, and then you will judge fairly" (3, 36). If a piece of cake is to be shared between two siblings, parents will sometimes have one child cut the piece in two and allow the other child to choose the first piece. In this way, the first child is taught to be fair in how he divides the treat and not give himself any advantage. Whether we are dealing with others in matters of business or in our personal lives, we should imagine the situation from the other person's perspective and treat him or her as we would wish to be treated. This is the meaning of "do unto others as you would have it done unto you" (see Matt. 7:12).

Another selfish inclination St. Francis warns against is the fostering of selfish desires. Here he does not mean the desire of evil or sinful things. "Everyone knows that we must avoid evil desires," he writes (3, 37). In this section of *An Introduction to the Devout Life*, he is concerned rather with the desire of good things that are unattainable or not proper to our state in life. Such desires do us more harm than good.

He gives the example of a married woman who desires to live a cloistered life as a nun, or a man who wishes to purchase property from a neighbor who has no intent to sell. Desiring things we cannot have or have no control over St. Francis considers useless and self-indulgent. He uses himself as another example:

> If when I am ill I give way to the wish to minister or preach, visit other sick persons or perform the duties of the healthy, are not my wishes fruitless, since it is not in my power to execute them? And meanwhile these useless wishes impede others which I ought to have—the wish to be very patient, very resigned, obedient, mortified, and gentle under my sufferings, which is what for the time being God requires of me. (3, 37)

Our desires serve as motivation, and when we waste time desiring things that are impossible for us, we render that motivation impotent; we may find we lack the motivation we should have for our proper duties. If a private in the marine corps spends all his time wishing he were a general, he'll never become a corporal or a lieutenant because he'll never have bothered to become a good private. If a married man longs for the life of a celibate priest, he is not being a good husband to his wife. If a priest fosters a desire for marriage and family life, he neglects the proper care of his flock.

Now, we all may wish we lived in different circumstances from time to time. A parent struggling to find a few moments of solitude in a house full of small children may momentarily envy the monk in his quiet cell. St. Francis is not speaking of such fleeting desires. "I am speaking," he writes, "of such desires as occupy the heart, for there is no harm in common wishes if they do not become habitual" (3, 37).

Even the desire for spiritual goods can become harmful if they are beyond our reach. The desire to serve God is good, but as St. Paul points out in his First Letter to the Corinthians, the Spirit gives us all different gifts for God's service. Some are given special wisdom, others gifts of healing, others prophecy. Some are called to be apostles, others teachers, and others administrators (see 1 Cor. 12:4–31). Desiring another's spiritual gifts is just as covetous as desiring another's property. If we long for gifts we don't have, it causes us to neglect the gifts we do possess. St. Francis instructs us to cultivate the spiritual gifts we have, whatever they might be.

We all must begin where we are and proceed from there. This requires humility, which is the best remedy against selfishness. St. Francis advises against wishing for large crosses until we've learned to bear the small crosses we already have. "It is a mistake to wish for martyrdom whilst we have not courage to endure a sharp word" (3, 37). I often point out to couples during marriage preparation that every husband likes to think he would take a bullet for his wife. But is he willing to wash the dishes? A desire for grand sacrifices is meaningless if we are not willing to make small ones.

Someone who has recently converted to the Faith may discover the great treasury of Catholic prayers and devotions and, recognizing that they are all good and worthy, seek to do them all. This is like jumping into the deep end of the pool before you learn to swim. It is enough for now to wade into the shallow end and get your feet wet. New converts might think that if they don't do so many holy hours, or pray a whole litany of novenas and chaplets, they are missing out on some essential aspect of devotion. Of course this is unreasonable, but the desire for all these good things can lead to frustration in the spiritual life. St. Francis likens it to eating too much food and getting indigestion. "Such an appetite [for spiritual devotion] is a good sign, but take care that you are able to digest all you would eat. With the help of your spiritual father select from amongst all such practices those which are suitable to you" (3, 37).

There are many ways to love and serve God and neighbor, and none of us can do them all. God doesn't expect us to. Whether in our professional life, personal life, or spiritual life, the idea that we "have to do it all" is a form of selfishness. Satan can easily use our spiritual pride against us. Indeed, it is his primary vice. "I do not bid you to put aside all good desires," St. Francis writes, "but only to regulate them; to execute those which are practicable at the present moment, and lay up those which are impractical in store for a fitting season" (3, 37).

Selfishness leads us to love ourselves first and everyone else (even God) as a distant second. Scripture provides a framework to give a proper order to our love: God first and then our neighbors as equal to ourselves. This properly ordered love helps us to temper and regulate our desires, ensuring that they are ordered toward serving God and not our own interests.

## Questions for Reflection

1. Do you find that your standards for others differ from your standards for yourself? Do you tend to judge others more harshly or more leniently?
2. Are there certain spiritual gifts you see in others that you find yourself coveting? What spiritual gifts might you possess that you are neglecting?
3. What is the relationship between selfishness and humility? How does this impact the daily decisions you are called to make?

## Scripture for Meditation

> LORD, my heart is not proud;
> nor are my eyes haughty.
> I do not busy myself with great matters,
> with things too sublime for me.
> Rather, I have stilled my soul,
> Like a weaned child to its mother,
> weaned is my soul.
> Israel, hope in the LORD,
> now and forever. (Ps. 131)

14

# Married Life: Part 1

Marriage is a sacrament. Any discourse on Christian marriage must begin with this understanding. Sacraments are efficacious signs of God's grace in this world (CCC 1131). That means they are signs that bring about what they signify—in this case, God's own divine life. Marriage is such a sign, meaning that Christian marriage should be an icon of God's love for us—more than an icon, an incarnation. As I mentioned in the earlier chapter on chastity, our bodies are more like the Eucharist than like bread. They are sacred, and marriage is the intimate union of two sacred bodies. Like the Eucharist, marriage begins by saying, "This is my body that is for you" (1 Cor. 11:24).

St. Francis de Sales calls marriage "all holy":

> Its institution, its end, its purpose, its form, and its matter, are all holy. It is the orchard of Christianity, which fills the world with the Faithful in order to fill up the number of the elect in Heaven, and it greatly concerns the public welfare that the sanctity of marriage, which is the source of all its well-being, be preserved inviolate. (3, 38)

Marriage is not a private matter of the bedroom. It concerns the public welfare, as St. Francis observes, because marriage is the foundation of family life, and families (not individuals) are the foundation of society.

To preserve the sanctity of marriage, we need first to understand the meaning and purpose of marriage, which is something our world is becoming increasingly confused about. Far from being a mere social construct, the Church understands marriage to be something written into our very nature as men and women, something we cannot change without violating our human dignity (CCC 1603). The Church recognizes two ends of marriage, mirroring the two ends of the sexual act identified in the chapter on chastity: "the good of the spouses and the procreation and education of offspring" (CCC 1601). St. John Chrysostom said that the purpose of marriage is "to make us chaste and to make us parents."[95] Respecting these two ends, the Church understands marriage by definition to include three characteristics: it is faithful, it is lifelong, and it is open to life (see CCC 1643-1654).

We live in a society that treats marriage, sex, and children as three separate goods that may be pursued independently of one another. Contraception allows us to have sex without children. Invitro fertilization and other reproductive technologies allow us to have children without sex. Because half of marriages end in divorce and many today forgo marriage altogether, many children are being raised outside of marriage. Widespread acceptance of divorce means that we've forgotten that marriage is meant to be faithful, just as widespread acceptance of contraception means that we've forgotten that marriage is meant to be fruitful. So what is marriage, then? When robbed of its fundamental meaning, it becomes a mere social convention. It is anything we say it is. Given this attitude, the acceptance of so-called same sex marriage was inevitable.

By contrast, the Catholic Church understands marriage, sex, and children to be aspects of one good—family life. You cannot separate one from the others without doing violence to the whole.

[95] St. John Chrysostom, *Sermon on Marriage*.

God's first command to the human race was to "be fruitful and multiply" (Gen. 1:28). St. Francis says that "the bringing of children into the world and multiplying the people is a good thing and very holy, for it is the principal end of marriage" (3, 39). Each and every human person is made in the image and likeness of God and will live forever. What an honor it is to be allowed to participate in God's act of creation! St. Francis de Sales rightly says that "it is a great honor to be permitted to increase the number of souls whom God will save, and who will serve him through all eternity" (3, 38).

St. Francis likens sexual intercourse to eating. Like sex, eating has two purposes. One is basic biology. We eat to nourish our bodies. The other purpose is social. We eat shared meals together to foster bonds of fellowship (the word *companion* means "one I break bread with"). Both purposes are important. Eating also happens to be quite enjoyable, praise God, but this is a secondary aspect, not essential to its nature. As long as I eat to nourish my body and build bonds of fellowship, then I have a healthy attitude toward food and can enjoy the pleasure of eating with a clear conscience. But if I eat primarily for pleasure without respect to its proper ends—if I eat out of boredom, convenience, or because I can't control my appetite—then I have a disordered attitude toward food. This is the sin of gluttony.

Likewise, sex has ends for the good of life and society: repro-duction and the union of the spouses. And like eating, sex is also enjoyable. But if we engage in sexual acts purely for pleasure or because we cannot control our appetites, without respect to its proper ends—even within marriage—then our attitude toward sex has become disordered. This is the sin of lust.

The reason the Church has always condemned contracep-tion (as did every Protestant church before 1930) is that it means pursuing the pleasure of sex while acting to disrupt its natural end, thereby doing violence to the meaning of the act. The same is true of any sexual act that is not ordered toward procreation. St. Francis de Sales declares that "since the bringing of children into the world is the principal end of marriage, to do anything in order to prevent the accomplishment of this end is always a mortal sin" (3, 39).

There is sometimes a misconception that the Church is of the opinion that every sexual act must lead to the conception of a child. This is untrue and a perversion of the Church's actual teaching. Natural Family Planning is a morally approved method of spacing children that takes advantage of the woman's natural fertility cycle. In a nutshell, while men's fertility is consistent, women are fertile for only a few days each month. It is possible to learn to recognize the biological signs that a woman is approaching her fertile period. Armed with this knowledge, a couple may choose to avoid or engage in sexual intercourse during that time, depending on whether they wish to conceive. (Note: this is not the "calendar" or "rhythm" method; there is a lot more science involved.)

It is sometimes suggested that married couples sin if they choose to abstain from sexual activity during the wife's fertile period without a serious reason. It is important to note that being open to life does not mean having as many children as physically possible. The Church entrusts this matter to the prudential judgment of the couple (there is no official list of approved reasons for avoiding pregnancy). If a couple chooses to avoid having children for selfish reasons, that is a sin of selfishness and not contraception. Nor does openness to life mean that every sexual act must end in conception. There is nothing wrong with couples coming together to express their spousal intimacy during infertile periods. St. Francis de Sales recognized no harm in married couples' engaging in intercourse "as faithfully and freely as if it were in the hopes of having children, although on some occasions there might be no such expectation" (3, 39).

When used to avoid pregnancy, Natural Family Planning has a success rate as good as or higher than most artificial contraceptive methods, and when used to achieve pregnancy, Natural Family Planning has been able to assist many couples struggling with infertility by helping them to maximize the chance of conception by targeting the wife's most fertile period. Perhaps most tellingly, couples who practice Natural Family Planning have an exceptionally low rate of divorce. I believe this is due to the fact that the method forces couples to have honest, regular discussions about their sex lives and whether it is prudent to welcome another child into their family at a given time. If couples learn to communicate well about these intimate matters, they avoid many of the conflicts that can lead to the breakdown of a marriage.

## Questions for Reflection

1. Think of some married couples who were positive influences on you when you were growing up. What did you admire about their relationships?
2. Do you think it is difficult to live the vocation of marriage in a society that has such a different understanding of marriage from that of the Church? What are some particular challenges?
3. What factors do you think contribute to the widespread practice of contraception today, even among those in the Church? How might those factors be mitigated?

## Scripture for Meditation

The husband should fulfill his duty toward his wife, and likewise the wife toward her husband. A wife does not have authority over her own body, but rather her husband, and similarly a husband does not have authority over his own body, but rather his wife. Do not deprive each other, except perhaps by mutual consent for a time, to be free for prayer. (1 Cor. 7:3–5)

# 15

# Married Life: Part 2

The last chapter dealt chiefly with procreation, or the physical union of the spouses in marriage. In this chapter, we will concern ourselves with spiritual union. Although procreation is identified by St. Francis de Sales as the principal end of marriage (3, 39), it is not its highest end. When St. John Chrysostom identified the two ends of marriage as "to make us chaste and to make us parents," he observed that "marriage does not always lead to child-bearing … so the purpose of chastity takes precedence."[96]

Like all sacraments, Marriage is meant to sanctify us. Most sacraments convey grace for the benefit of the recipient, but two of the sacraments, Marriage and Holy Orders, convey grace for the benefit of others. Holy Orders conveys grace for the good of the Church, and Matrimony conveys graces for the good of one's spouse and children. Put simply, the primary concern of the married person is to help his or her spouse get to Heaven.

What makes a Christian marriage different from other marriages—what makes it a sacrament—is the presence of Christ. When a baptized man marries a baptized woman, it is a marriage between not two people but three (really five, as Christ does nothing without the Father and the Holy Spirit). As St. Paul says, " I live, no longer I, but Christ lives in me" (Gal. 2:20). When the Christ-in-me marries the Christ-in-you, then Christ is made present in the world in a new

---

[96] St. John Chrysostom, *Sermon on Marriage*.

way through our union. "Their mutual love becomes an image of the absolute and unfailing love with which God loves man" (CCC 1604). "Would that our Blessed Savior were always invited to all marriage-feasts, as to that of Cana," St. Francis implores (3, 38).

Christian couples should approach marriage as an intentional vocation ordered toward holiness. "Marriage," the *Catechism* states, "helps us to overcome self-absorption, egoism, [and] pursuit of one's own pleasure" (1609). There is no room in marriage for jealousy. "It is a vain imagination that love is exalted by jealousy," St. Francis writes. "It may testify that love is great, but not that it is good, pure, and perfect; since the perfection of love presupposes confidence in the virtue of what we love, whereas jealousy presupposes lack of confidence" (3, 38). As St. Paul states, "Love is patient, love is kind. It is not jealous, [love] is not pompous, it is not inflated, it is not rude, it does not seek its own interests" (1 Cor. 13:4–5). So should Christian marriage be. It provides the context in which husbands and wives are called to practice all the virtues, including obedience, humility, patience, temperance, and especially charity.

The Ven. Patrick Peyton, known as "the Rosary priest," coined the phrase "the family that prays together stays together." Prayer should be at the heart of Christian marriage. "There is no union so precious and so fruitful between husband and wife as that of holy devotion," St. Francis writes, "in which they should mutually lead and sustain each other" (3, 38). St. Francis suggests that instead of celebrating their anniversaries with "worldly feasting," couples should "dedicate that day to Confession and Communion, and more than ordinarily fervent prayer; commending their married life to God, and renewing their resolutions of sanctifying it by mutual faithfulness and love" (3, 39). Indeed, the Church recommends that married couples renew their vows, especially on the occasion of significant anniversaries.

Being intentional about their vocation means that spouses talk regularly about their marriage and pray together, both as a couple and as a family with their children. It would be a good idea to take retreats together from time to time, perhaps annually, as a way of keeping their marriage focused on Christ.

The most beautiful and perhaps most misunderstood Scripture passage about marriage is Ephesians 5:21–33. The part of this passage most people remember (especially husbands) is St. Paul's instruction that "wives should be subordinate to their husbands as to the Lord" (Eph. 5:22). Reading this verse out of context gives only a partial and distorted view of Christian matrimony.

We must note, first of all, that St. Paul begins his instruction for married couples by saying, "Be subordinate to one another out of reverence for Christ" (Eph. 5:21). This call for mutual subjugation is the lens through which the rest of this passage should be viewed. Yes, wives are subject to their husbands, and husbands are subject to their wives, in different but complementary ways. Thus, both are called to grow in the virtue of obedience. The wife is subject to her husband as the Church is subject to Christ. The husband, for his part, is called to subject himself to his wife "even as Christ loved the Church and handed himself over for her" (Eph. 5:25). Any husband who reads this passage and thinks he's getting off easy hasn't spent enough time in front of a crucifix. Christ is Head of the Church but not in a domineering fashion. He reminds us that He came not to be served but to serve and to give His life for His Bride (see Matt. 20:28). Both husbands and wives are called to participate in the sacrifice of Christ through their shared marital vocation. Neither is master; both are servants of the other.

The *Catechism* teaches, "It is by following Christ, renouncing themselves, and taking up their crosses that spouses will be able to 'receive' the original meaning of marriage and live it with the help of Christ. This grace of Christian marriage is a fruit of Christ's cross, the source of all Christian life" (1615). Sometimes the cross we bear will be our spouse. A priest once asked the participants at a retreat to lift up their crosses for him to bless. One woman lifted up her husband, saying, "He is my cross." We laugh at the joke, but it is our crosses that lead the way to Heaven.

St. Paul ends this passage with these words: "This is a great mystery, but I speak in reference to Christ and the Church" (Eph. 5:32). Everything Paul says about marriage is an image of how Christ, the Bridegroom, binds Himself to the Church, His Bride. Marriage is the key to understanding how God relates to His Church. The New Covenant is a marriage covenant. The reason God is a "He" is because the Church is a "she." If we don't understand marriage, we don't understand our relationship to God.

This makes marriage a very high calling. St. John Chrysostom, who wrote more on marriage than any other Father of the Church, went so far as to say, "It is possible for us to surpass all others in virtue by becoming good husbands and wives." Marriage concretizes our vocation of holiness in a particular state in life, in a particular family, with a particular spouse. As I advise couples I prepare for marriage, from the moment you say, "I do," the measure of love you offer your spouse is the measure of love you offer to God.

St. John Chrysostom counsels husbands to have this attitude toward their wives (which wives should also have toward their husbands): "Tell her that you love her more than your own life, because this present life is nothing, and that your only hope is that the two of you pass through this life in such a way that in the world to come you will be united in perfect love.... If your marriage is like this, your perfection will rival the holiest of monks."[97]

---

[97] St. John Chrysostom, *Homily 20*.

## Questions for Reflection

1. How do married couples, both those with children and those without, pursue the ends of marriage in their vocations? What are some different considerations for each situation?
2. If you are married, what sacrifices are you called to make in order to help your spouse get to Heaven?
3. What do you think it means for married couples to be mutually subject to each other? What sort of respect and humility does this call for in married life?

## Scripture for Meditation

Be subordinate to one another out of reverence for Christ. Wives should be subordinate to their husbands as to the Lord. For the husband is head of his wife just as Christ is head of the church, he himself the savior of the body. As the church is subordinate to Christ, so wives should be subordinate to their husbands in everything. Husbands, love your wives, even as Christ loved the church and handed himself over for her to sanctify her, cleansing her by the bath of water with the word, that he might present to himself the church in splendor, without spot or wrinkle or any such thing, that she might be holy and without blemish. So [also] husbands should love their wives as their own bodies. He who loves his wife loves himself. For no one hates his own flesh but rather nourishes and cherishes it, even as Christ does the church, because we are members of his body.

For this reason a man shall leave [his] father
  and [his] mother
  and be joined to his wife,
  and the two shall become one flesh.

This is a great mystery, but I speak in reference to Christ and the church. (Eph. 5:21–32)

# 16

# Single Life

Marriage brings with it many opportunities to grow less selfish and more charitable simply by reason of the shared life of the family. Learning to live peacefully in common with others has a way of smoothing the rough edges of our personalities. Marriage also provides built-in avenues of service in the daily ways we give time and attention to our spouses and children. The key to advancing in virtue as a single person is not to allow yourself to become selfish but to seek opportunities to give yourself in service of God and neighbor.

There are two ways of being single in the world: being merely unmarried and being celibate. Those who are merely unmarried remain open to being married in the future; those who have made vows or promises of celibacy have committed themselves to remaining unmarried for the sake of the Lord.

St. Francis cautions those who are unmarried but intend to be married to "preserve with jealousy your first love for your [spouse]" (3, 41). For all of the reasons described in previous chapters, sexual intercourse before marriage is immoral. But unmarried people would also do well to avoid rash emotional or spiritual intimacy with their dating partners before such time as they are married. Much heartbreak in romance comes from committing our hearts to another before such commitment is warranted. For this reason, it is good to avoid all forms of intimacy that are beyond the actual state of the relationship. In other words, don't treat someone as your spouse, either with your body or your heart, until he or she actually becomes so.

Dating should be approached as vocational discernment. Marriage is entered into by free choice, but once that choice is made, it is a lifelong commitment, "for better or for worse." Dating is a time to learn about your potential mate and discover how your personalities, temperaments, hearts, and minds correspond to each other. Beyond figuring out whether you are attracted to that person, dating should help you to discern whether you can trust him or her. Is he or she reliable? Dependable? Is this someone you want to spend your life with, to share in your joys and sorrows, triumphs and tragedies? Save your heart for that person, and you will do well.

But what of those who have no intention to marry? In the holy Gospels, our Lord speaks of those who choose celibacy "for the sake of the kingdom" and says, "Whoever can accept this ought to accept it" (Matt. 19:12). What does it mean to be celibate for the sake of the kingdom? Whether one is unmarried by choice or by accident (i.e., a widow or a widower), being celibate for the sake of the kingdom means living your life not in hopes of marriage but in the hope of the Lord. St. Paul points out that a married man is concerned with pleasing his wife, but an unmarried man is concerned with pleasing the Lord; likewise, a married woman is concerned with pleasing her husband, but an unmarried woman "is anxious about the things of the Lord, so that she may be holy in both body and spirit" (1 Cor. 7:32–34).

In his advice to widows, St. Francis de Sales similarly distinguishes between widows who seek to be married again (whom he says cannot be blamed) and those who have chosen to embrace widowhood as their permanent state in life as a means of serving the Lord. These he calls widows "not only in body, but in heart"

(3, 40). St. Paul refers to these latter as being "truly widows" in his first letter to Timothy. "The real widow, who is all alone, has set her hope on God and continues in supplications and prayers night and day" (1 Tim. 5:5). St. Francis says, "This renunciation of a second marriage must be done in purity and simplicity, so as to center all affections more wholly in God." If a widow has young children to care for, she needs to care for her children, he advises, but if her children are grown, that leaves the widow more free to apply "all her thoughts and affections ... to her advancement in the love of God" (3, 40).

"Prayer should be the widow's continual exercise," he writes.

> Let her serve the poor and sick, console the afflicted, lead maidens toward a devout life, and set a perfect example of virtue to all young wives. Necessity and simplicity are the ornaments of their attire, humility and chastity of their deeds, purity and cheerfulness of their words, modesty and meekness of their eyes; and Jesus Christ crucified is the sole love of their heart. (3, 40)

Everything St. Francis writes of widows would apply equally to widowers who choose to remain in that state for the sake of God and to better serve the Lord.

The single life leaves one free in many regards. Those embracing a celibate vocation choose to use that freedom to serve not themselves but God. There are many ways of doing this, be it in the priesthood, as a monastic or consecrated religious, a widow or widower, or a consecrated single person. But like marriage, celibate vocations also require commitment.

Celibacy gives a powerful witness to the world that our relationship with God is enough. The celibate person lives his or her life already in anticipation of the resurrection, when we will neither marry nor be given in marriage but will be like the angels in Heaven (Matt. 22:30). Though there is no marriage in Heaven, we will not be alone. Heaven is communion, and the Church is a community. We need community and human relationships to sustain us in our vocations. This is why those who choose to renounce the world for the sake of the kingdom generally do so in monasteries and religious orders, whereas hermits are relatively rare. Those without the benefit of such society are well advised to foster relationships with others who share their state in life. Priests should seek the friendship of fellow priests, widows should support one another in their widowhood, and all single people ought to know the love and support of the Church.

## Questions for Reflection

1. What is the difference between simply being single and being celibate "for the sake of the kingdom"?
2. What do single people need to be mindful of to avoid falling into selfishness? If you are single, whom are you called to serve?
3. If you are single or celibate, who are helping you along your journey to Heaven? Where do you find community and sustaining friendships?

## Scripture for Meditation

I should like you to be free of anxieties. An unmarried man is anxious about the things of the Lord, how he may please the Lord. But a married man is anxious about the things of the world, how he may please his wife, and he is divided. An unmarried woman or a virgin is anxious about the things of the Lord, so that she may be holy in both body and spirit. A married woman, on the other hand, is anxious about the things of the world, how she may please her husband. (1 Cor. 7:32–34)

Part IV

# Weeding Out Temptation

# 1

## Worldly Opinions

When we first devote ourselves to the pursuit of holiness through intentional discipleship, we may feel marked out from the world and even from other Christians. This can become a temptation for us to turn from the path of devotion and back to our former way of life. The remedy prescribed by St. Francis de Sales is to have faith and persevere.

We can expect the world to have a negative opinion of us if we follow the path of Christian devotion. They "will pronounce your altered ways to be hypocrisy, affectation, or bigotry," St. Francis says (4, 1). We might imagine that in the past, all the world was Christian and took the Faith seriously, but the attitudes St. Francis says the world will have against us are the same then as they are now, though perhaps for different reasons. Christians have always been a people set apart, especially those who take their Faith seriously.

Hypocrisy was the chief sin of which Jesus accused the Pharisees of His day. To be a hypocrite is to say one thing while doing another. The Pharisees took seriously the practice of religion—at least the outward show of it. It is not uncommon, even within the Church, for those who similarly take the practice of religion seriously to be called pharisaical (that is to say, hypocritical), whether they are sincere in their devotion or not. Let us be assured that the Pharisees' fault was not in their outward show of devotion but in their lack of interior devotion. If our external devotion corresponds to a genuine interior disposition, we can ignore accusations of hypocrisy.

Perhaps people have known other Christians to be hypocrites, and so they believe all Christians to be hypocrites. All we can do is apologize for the failures of these members of the Body of Christ, do penance for them, and strive to be a contrasting example of sincere devotion. You can also point to the saints as counterexamples. We judge a sport not by its worst athletes but by its best. The saints are our champions. They have run the race and won the crown (see 1 Cor. 9:24). Their lives show us what perseverance in the Faith can attain.

Some may accuse you of affectation, of putting on a show of piety in an attempt to appear holier than you really are. Others will accuse you of bigotry. This is especially common today in the moral arena, in which the Church's values run counter to those of the world. Moral relativism has become the accepted norm. The world holds that we have the right to define for ourselves what is morally good or bad (if we even hold to those categories at all). Therefore, if you uphold the Church's timeless teaching that some moral acts are objectively evil, you will be called a bigot and be accused of "forcing your religion" upon others.

This is truer of some moral teachings than of others. You will be praised for upholding the Christian duty to care for the poor because the world likes to appear compassionate. But you will be accused of narrow-mindedness, backwards thinking, bigotry, or worse if you suggest that contraception is wrong, abortion is evil, or same-sex marriage is a fiction. The world likes Christians, as long as they follow only those tenets of the Faith that the world approves and don't take their Christianity too seriously.

Moreover, you will most likely have your own interior doubts. You may feel unworthy because you continue to struggle with habitual sin. You may feel frustrated that the fruits of your devotion seem small or slow-growing. You may look at our Lord, the Blessed Mother, and the saints and know yourself to be unworthy by comparison. Do the cries of hypocrisy ring true? Is your piety just an affectation? Are you being too judgmental in upholding unpopular Church teachings?

Being an intentional disciple of Jesus Christ can be difficult. It means a change of life for us, and all change is hard at first. St. Francis predicts this. "It is very probable," he writes, "that you will have sundry inward struggles in the course of your altered life … [that] you will have some sad and discouraging feelings: if so, only be patient, they will come to nothing" (4, 2).

The psalmist asks, "Who may go up the mountain of the LORD? Who can stand in his holy place?" (Ps. 24:3). St. Francis says, "But as you gaze upon the steep mountain of Christian perfection: 'Alas!' you exclaim, 'how shall I ever ascend it?' Be of good cheer" (4, 2). We are but beginners. What matters for now is not how high we have climbed, only that we are climbing. Don't give heed to the voices calling for us to descend.

"The one who perseveres to the end will be saved" (Matt. 24:13). "Believe me," St. Francis writes, "with perseverance you will not fail to receive such deeply delicious and heartfelt satisfactions, that you will own [that] the world offers you only gall as compared with this honey, and that one day of devotion is worth more than a thousand years of worldly gratification" (4, 2).

As St. Francis rightly reminds us, "Whatever we do, the world will find fault" (4, 2). It has always been this way. Remember that our Lord had to deal with His detractors and promised for His followers persecution along with eternal life. "Blessed are you when they insult you and persecute you and utter every kind of evil against you [falsely] because of me. Rejoice and be glad, for your reward will be great in heaven" (Matt. 5:11-12).

What matters is not what the world thinks of us but only what God thinks of us. The world can neither condemn nor save us.

Jesus says, "If the world hates you, realize that it hated me first. If you belonged to the world, the world would love its own; but because you do not belong to the world, and I have chosen you out of the world, the world hates you" (John 15:18–19).

"We are crucified to the world, and the world should be crucified to us," says St. Francis. "It counts us as fools, let us count its votaries as madmen" (4, 1).

## Questions for Reflection

1. Have you ever been accused of hypocrisy because of your practice of the Faith? How did you respond?
2. Does holiness seem out of reach much of the time? Do the examples of the saints seem attainable?
3. Jesus predicts persecution for those who follow Him. How can you avoid falling into the sin of spiritual pride when you are persecuted for your Faith?

## Scripture for Meditation

Then to what shall I compare the people of this generation? What are they like? They are like children who sit in the marketplace and call to one another,

> "We played the flute for you, but you did not dance.
> We sang a dirge, but you did not weep."

For John the Baptist came neither eating food nor drinking wine, and you said, "He is possessed by a demon." The Son of Man came eating and drinking and you said, "Look, he is a glutton and a drunkard, a friend of tax collectors and sinners." But wisdom is vindicated by all her children. (Luke 7:31–35)

## 2

# The Nature of Temptation

Before we commit any sin, we first experience the temptation to sin; yet the temptation itself is not sinful. This is a point on which many are often confused. In the Lord's Prayer, for example, some wonder why we should pray "lead us not into temptation," assuming that God would never lead anyone to be tempted. But Scripture tells us that God led His own Son into temptation. "Jesus ... was led by the Spirit into the desert for forty days, to be tempted by the devil" (Luke 4:1–2). The Spirit of God led Jesus to be tempted, yet we know Jesus did not sin.

St. Francis de Sales illustrates the relationship between sin and temptation using the example of a princess who is happily married to her husband. An enamored nobleman sends a messenger to her with a proposition against her virtue. Three things then occur. The messenger arrives. The princess either gives the messenger an audience or sends him away. Finally, she either accepts or rejects the proposition. If the princess rejects the messenger or his proposition, she does nothing blameworthy. Only if she accepts the proposition does she sin.

To use a more contemporary example, we might imagine a husband who is traveling away from home on business. After dining by himself and paying the bill, the attractive waitress writes her phone number on his receipt with an invitation to call her while he is in town. This makes him feel a certain way; perhaps he is flattered, perhaps amused, or perhaps offended. However he may feel, he has a decision to make. Does he call her or not? Does he accept her invitation?

St. Francis names these three degrees by which we fall into sin as temptation, delectation, and consent. Temptation is only the initial invitation to sin. The invitation makes us feel a certain way. But only when we give our consent is the sin consummated. We are not responsible for having received the invitation, and we are not responsible for how it may or may not make us feel. We are responsible for our choices.

Obviously, it is easier for us to resist temptation if the invitation holds little or no attraction for us. If the princess in St. Francis's example refuses to give the messenger an audience, it is unlikely she will accept the proposition he carries. If the traveling husband is deeply committed to his wife, he will be able to resist his temptation with very little effort. But let's imagine that his marriage is on the rocks. He has been feeling lonely and insecure. The proposition, which he knows to be wrong, is nevertheless flattering to him. It will take greater strength of will on his part to resist the temptation, but he can still resist it. St. Francis encourages us to "be brave amidst temptations ... keeping clearly in mind the difference between feeling them and consenting to them" (4, 3).

It is possible when temptation comes our way for us to find pleasure and displeasure in it simultaneously. This is because, St. Francis says, "our soul has two natures, one inferior and the other superior, and the former will not always obey the latter but takes its own course; so sometimes the inferior takes pleasure in temptation without the consent and contrary to the will of the superior" (4, 3). The superior part of our soul involves our rational intellect and free will, whereas the inferior part relates to our baser desires, which are often outside our control.

Let's say you have decided to go on a diet to lose weight. Your rational mind knows and accepts that this means you cannot eat cake, even though it is your favorite dessert. So when someone shows up at the office with a cake to celebrate a coworker's birthday, it is a real temptation for you. The cake smells delicious. It's chocolate—your favorite flavor! You can imagine how it would taste, and your mouth begins to water. You cannot control any of this. But despite the appeal, you know you shouldn't have any, and so you politely turn down the slice that is offered you. The cake invokes pleasurable feelings, but also displeasure, because you know the attraction you feel toward the cake runs counter to your weight-loss goal and needs to be resisted.

This is why the spiritual discipline of fasting is recommended by the Church. Denying ourselves a good that we desire helps us learn to keep the higher powers of our soul in charge and not let our base desires run the show. According to St. Francis, the fact that these two aspects of our soul can often be at odds is what St. Paul refers to when he writes, "I see in my members another principle at war with the law of my mind" (Rom. 7:23), and "For the flesh has desires against the Spirit, and the Spirit against the flesh; these are opposed to each other, so that you may not do what you want" (Gal. 5:17).

Obviously, it is preferable that the temptation to sin would hold little or no attraction for us because then temptation would be easier to resist. It would mean that even our base desires had become aligned to the will of God, and nothing displeasing to God would hold any attraction for us. This is what Heaven will be like, when all aspects of our being will have been perfected. But while we sojourn here on earth, we must continue to battle against the world, the flesh, and the devil—the three sources of temptation.

There can be great virtue in resisting temptation that holds a strong attraction for us. It is no praiseworthy thing for someone to turn down a drink if alcohol turns his stomach. But for a recovering alcoholic to turn down the same drink is a more meritorious act because it takes a greater force of will. As I mentioned in the previous section, in the chapter on "Choosing Virtue," each of us suffers from certain vices more than others. Not only will we naturally experience temptation in these areas more frequently from the world and the flesh, because of our disposition, but the devil will intentionally assault us where our defenses are weak (he is both smart and lazy). Just as it is unwise for a recovering alcoholic to visit bars, we should develop an awareness of our principal vices and be especially on guard against them by avoiding near occasions of these sins.

St. Francis de Sales warns, however, that it is possible to sin without consenting fully to the temptation if we intentionally or neglectfully place ourselves in situations that we know will tempt us (assuming they can be avoided). He uses himself as an example. "I know that if I play [games] I easily lose my temper and use bad language, and that play is a temptation to me. In such case I sin whenever I play, and I am guilty of whatever temptations may injure me in so doing." As good stewards of our souls, we should do what we can to avoid temptations we can anticipate. So when you are tempted, St. Francis says to "reflect whether you have voluntarily brought it on yourself ... whether you might have avoided the occasion, or have foreseen the temptation" (4, 6). We are responsible for the temptations we experience to the extent that we are able to avoid them.

Similarly, we incur guilt if we intentionally delight in the pleasure temptation brings, even if we do not consent to the act itself. A fleeting attraction that involuntarily arises from temptation is not sinful if we do our best not to linger in it. But if we "voluntarily and with deliberation" make a conscious choice to enjoy the temptation, "such deliberate resolution is a grievous sin, supposing that the object of delectation is mortally sinful" (4, 6). Thus, if the traveling husband spent the night fantasizing about a lurid affair with the waitress, he has yielded to temptation in his heart, and our Lord warns that this is just as deadly to the soul. "I say to you, everyone who looks at a woman with lust has already committed adultery with her in his heart" (Matt. 5:28). "There is impurity in allowing either heart or body to consent to what is impure; and impurity consists so entirely in the consent of the heart, that without it the consent of the body cannot be sin" (4, 6).

Many temptations will arise that we can in no way avoid, and St. Francis says we should not despair over this. "These grievous assaults and powerful temptations are never permitted by God save to those whom He purposes to exalt in His pure and excellent love.... Whatever temptations, then, assault you, and whatever attraction ensues, so long as your will refuses to consent to either, be not afraid, God is not displeased" (4, 5).

Temptation is not itself a sin, but only the opportunity to sin. And an opportunity to sin is also an opportunity to be faithful. It is an opportunity to say no to Satan and yes to God, just as Jesus did during His temptation in the desert. Jesus endured His temptation so that we might have the strength to endure ours, even if it lasts our lifetime, as St. Paul had to contend with his "thorn in the flesh" (2 Cor. 12:7). We don't know the specific nature of St. Paul's vexation, only that it was something he struggled with for quite some time.

Although he suffered from his temptation, St. Paul understood that it was something permitted by God and was therefore for his good. Despite his great spiritual gifts that might otherwise lead to pride, his temptation allowed Paul to remain humble, reminding him of his reliance upon God. "Three times I begged the Lord about this, that it might leave me," Paul writes, "but he said to me, 'My grace is sufficient for you, for power is made perfect in weakness'" (2 Cor. 12:8–9). In the midst of our strongest temptations, let us remember that God will not try us beyond our strength; "with the trial he will also provide a way out, so that you may be able to bear it" (1 Cor. 10:13).

## Questions for Reflection

1. Can you identify your primary sources of temptation? What might you do to avoid these situations, if possible?
2. How do you perceive the difference between experiencing the fleeting pleasure of temptation and indulging in the pleasure of temptation? Why is the latter sinful?
3. How might thinking of temptations as opportunities to be faithful change how you deal with them?

## Scripture for Meditation

I discover the principle that when I want to do right, evil is at hand. For I take delight in the law of God, in my inner self, but I see in my members another principle at war with the law of my mind, taking me captive to the law of sin that dwells in my members. Miserable one that I am! Who will deliver me from this mortal body? Thanks be to God through Jesus Christ our Lord. Therefore, I myself, with my mind, serve the law of God but, with my flesh, the law of sin. (Rom. 7:21–25)

3

# Resisting Temptation

Although we should do what we can to avoid the temptations we are able to foresee, temptations will nevertheless arise that we are unable to avoid. These we are called to resist.

The first measure in resisting temptation is to seek the help of God. If we think that we must resist all temptation by the sheer force of our will, we will fail. St. Francis de Sales compares the soul facing temptation to a child who encounters a bear in the woods. The first thing the child does is to call for the help of his parents. Likewise, we should not hesitate to call on God. "Turn your heart towards Jesus Christ crucified," St. Francis advises, "and making an act of love to Him, kiss His sacred feet. This is the best way of overcoming the enemy, whether in little or great temptations." It is good that we should accustom ourselves to doing this whenever temptation arises. Remember, the devil wants to draw us away from God. If "he perceives that his temptations only provoke us the more to that divine love," St. Francis explains, "he will cease to attack us" (4, 9).

If the big temptations we face can be compared to bears, St. Francis says the small ones might be compared to flies or gnats. "Doubtless bears and wolves are more dangerous than flies, but they do not cause us so much annoyance and irritation" (4, 8). I've lived close to the Smoky Mountain National Park for my entire adult life and have only rarely seen bears. But I encounter flies nearly every time I step outside (and not infrequently inside).

These smaller temptations are still dangerous because they are more common. Yielding to any one may not be a great matter, but they can weaken us over time by their sheer number.

St. Francis writes:

> It is an easy thing to abstain from murder, but it is very difficult to avoid those angry outbursts which are incessantly aroused within us. It is an easy thing to abstain from adultery, but it is not so easy to be wholly and ceaselessly pure in word, look, thought, and deed; an easy matter not to steal what belongs to another, but harder never to long after and covet it; easy not to bear legal false witness, but hard never to tell lies in our ordinary conversation. (4, 8)

Keeping the commandments is no great burden. The rich young man boasted to Jesus that he has kept the commandments all his life (Matt. 19:20; Luke 18:21). He had not committed idolatry, dishonored his parents, committed murder or adultery, or lied to or stolen from his neighbor. So he was not a complete jerk. Jesus calls us to greater things than merely not being sociopaths. He calls us to holiness. This is why He is concerned with matters of the heart. It is not enough simply not to murder or commit adultery. We should not hate or lust. Our Lord calls us to eradicate the seeds of sin in our heart before they take root and grow (see Matt. 5:21–30). Thus, we should diligently resist small temptations as well as large ones. And if we habitually resist the small ones, the large ones won't be as tempting.

St. Francis says the most effective way to combat these small daily temptations is by "not allowing them to torment us; for although they annoy us, they cannot do us any real harm so long as we are firm in our resolution to serve God.... Let them hum and buzz about your ears as they will, and attend to them no more than you would to flies" (4, 9). Don't waste time arguing with the devil, St. Francis advises. Just give him the same answer Jesus offered during His temptation. "Get away, Satan!...The Lord, your God, shall you worship and him alone shall you serve" (Matt. 4:10) (4, 9). Let this answer be sufficient.

Meanwhile, "divert your mind by some useful, praiseworthy work, for as this enters and occupies your heart, it will banish temptations and evil thoughts" (4, 7). Idle hands are the devil's workshop. An idle mind is his playground.

A more long-term strategy in learning to resist temptation involves seeking spiritual direction:

> The chief remedy against all temptations, great and small is to unfold the heart, and lay all its suggestions, inclinations, and feelings before our director; for you may observe that the first pledge which Satan seeks to gain from the soul he seduces, is that of silence. (4, 7)

The devil does not want us to talk about the evil desires in our hearts. If we never admit them to others, it becomes easy not to admit them to ourselves. Thus, we never deal with them, and they are allowed to grow.

Spiritual direction is different from Confession. In sacramental Confession, what is important is to name your sins, repent of them, and receive absolution. Spiritual direction allows you to go deeper; not just "these are my sins" but "these are my sinful inclinations." What temptations vex me in particular? From where do they arise? What aspects of my heart lead certain things to tempt me more than others? Why am I attracted to certain sins in this way? These are all questions that a spiritual director can help you to discern, but you must first be willing to unveil your heart dispassionately to him. If you are unable to find a good spiritual director, similar guidance can be found from a good confessor if you take care to confess not only sins committed in act but the sinful inclinations of your heart that make certain temptations difficult for you.

In either case, it is important for you to examine your heart to discern your particular weaknesses. As I mentioned in the last chapter, we each have our particular vices. No one is equally vicious in all areas. One person is more inclined to pride, another to sloth or envy. Growing in holiness requires self-knowledge. You should therefore, St. Francis writes, "from time to time examine what passions predominate in your soul, and having ascertained them, let your way of life be altogether opposed to them in thought, word, and deed" (4, 10).

Take these disordered passions to prayer and consider how they are affecting you. Consider, especially, what value they will hold upon your death:

> If you know that you have a tendency to vanity, often reflect on the misery of our present life, how these vanities will weigh upon your conscience on your deathbed, how unworthy they are of a noble heart, that they are a childish thing, and so forth.... If you are disposed to avarice, often reflect on the folly of this sin, which makes us the slave of that which is destined only to be our servant: remember that when death comes you must forsake all, and leave your riches in the hands of those who will squander them. (4, 10)

After reminding yourself of how foolish your vices are, you must "carefully practice the opposite virtue: and if occasions do not present themselves, go out of your way to seek them." If you are predisposed to pride, perform frequent acts of humility; if you are predisposed to greed, find ways to be generous; and so forth. "Thus you will strengthen your heart against future temptation" (4, 10).

## Questions for Reflection

1. What are the "flies and gnats" of temptations that vex you the most? Do you regularly confess these desires of your heart, even if you don't give in to them?
2. What is the opposite virtue of your primary vice? Think of some ways to put that virtue into practice.
3. What are some things you might do to occupy your mind and heart to help you resist temptations that arise from idleness?

## Scripture for Meditation

Where do the wars and where do the conflicts among you come from? Is it not from your passions that make war within your members?... So submit yourselves to God. Resist the devil, and he will flee from you. Draw near to God, and he will draw near to you. (James 4:1, 7–8)

# 4

# Worry and Sadness

Two things that can greatly trouble a soul and lead to many temptations are worry and sadness. I use the terms *worry* and *sadness* instead of *anxiety* and *depression* because the latter are most often used today to refer to clinical disorders, which are not what St. Francis de Sales has in mind, even though some English translations of his work use the word *anxiety*.

The difference between ordinary worry and sadness and clinical anxiety and depression has to do with the cause and the remedy. If anxiety and depression are psychological conditions resulting from trauma or some physiological cause, they need to be treated by a competent therapist, who may prescribe appropriate medication. Christians should not be reluctant to seek professional mental health any more than they would avoid seeing a doctor if they were suffering from a physical ailment. There has been a reluctance, or even suspicion, surrounding psychological therapy, rising from the false belief that people should be able to simply "get over" their mental illness. The problem is all in one's head, the thinking goes, and therefore imaginary. Or we tend to overspiritualize mental illness, thinking that if only we were holy enough, we wouldn't have these problems. This is simply not true. Thankfully, we now have a greater understanding that mental health issues, including anxiety and depression, are very real and can be treated if properly diagnosed.

Mental health does, of course, affect spiritual health, just as physical health can affect spiritual health. Mind, body, and soul are all integrated parts of the human person. When one is not well, the whole person is not well. If you receive a diagnosis of cancer, it is appropriate to talk with your pastor or spiritual director about spiritual concerns that stem from your illness and certainly to pray for healing. But you also need to see an oncologist. Doing so does not indicate a lack of faith. God often works through the hands of doctors and nurses. Similarly, if you suffer from anxiety, depression, or any other mental illness, it is good to speak with your pastor or spiritual director about how your mental illness is affecting your spiritual life, to pray for deliverance, and to receive appropriate guidance. But you should also be receiving care from a mental health professional.

From time to time, everyone experiences worry and sadness that do not arise from clinical conditions. It is possible for these afflictions to disturb our souls, and St. Francis offers simple guidance to help us address these ordinary emotions.

Worry or anxiety is a "disquietude" of the soul, and sadness is "that mental pain which is caused by the involuntary evils which affect us" (4, 11). When we are subject to evils—be they external things, such as poverty or illness, or internal things, such as temptation or spiritual dryness—it is normal for us to want to be delivered of them.

> If the soul seeks means to be delivered from her ill for the love of God, she will seek them with patience, gentleness, humility and tranquility, expecting to obtain her deliverance more from the goodness and providence of God than from her own labor, industry or diligence; if she seeks her deliverance from motives of self-love, she will be eager and heated in her search for means of deliverance, as if it depended more upon herself than upon God. (4, 11)[98]

[98] Ross translation.

This can cause us to feel frustrated and helpless. We become impatient with our situation. "Thus you see," he writes, "how an uneasiness which in the beginning is justifiable, engenders disquietude, which in its turn brings on an increase of anxiety which is highly dangerous" (4, 11).

The desire to be delivered from evils is good, but disquietude grows from "an ill-regulated desire to be delivered from the evil we experience." St. Francis advises, "If you earnestly desire to be delivered from some evil, or to attain to some good, above all things calm and tranquilize your mind, and compose your judgment and will; then quietly and gently pursue your aim, adopting suitable means with some method" (4, 11) trusting that God will bring you to the good you seek in the proper time and will care for you along the way.

When the disciples were in the storm-rocked boat, fearing that they might perish, Jesus was taking a nap. They woke Him up, incredulous. "Teacher," they cried, "do you not care that we are perishing?" Jesus woke up and rebuked the wind, saying to it, "Quiet! Be still!" Then He rebuked the disciples. "Why are you terrified? Do you not yet have faith?" (Mark 4:35–41). The troubles of our lives can be like a stormy sea that rocks our boat. When sailors experience rough waters, the way they keep from getting seasick is to keep their eye on a fixed point, such as the horizon. Let Jesus be our fixed point. Let Him be our safe harbor in whatever storms we experience. When you feel troubled, St. Francis says, you should "examine whether your heart is under your control" or if you have lost control due to "some ill-regulated emotion." "If it has strayed," he writes, "softly lead it back into the presence of God."

Sadness can be good or bad, and it arises from multiple causes. When you experience sadness, it is good to examine why you feel sad. If you feel sad because sad things have happened to you, that is normal and healthy. If you feel sad for no reason, that is depression, and you should seek professional treatment. If you feel sorrow over sins you have committed, that is guilt, which should lead you to repentance. If you feel guilty for no reason, that is scrupulosity and requires a different remedy.

Sadness is a spiritual pain. Like physical pain, it is good and useful as an indication that something is wrong. Pain leads us to identify and address the cause of the pain. So sadness should lead us to identify and address the cause of our sadness. All kinds of things can lead to sadness—large things, such as the loss of a loved one, or small things, such as an overcast day. What we want to avoid is becoming lost in our sadness. "Do not give in to sadness," Scripture tells us. "Grief has killed many, and nothing is to be gained from resentment" (Sir. 30:21, 23).

"Satan delights in sadness and melancholy," St. Francis points out, "since he himself is sad and melancholy, and will be so for all eternity, a condition which he would have all to share with him" (4, 11). Satan can use our genuine sadness to lead us into despair and spiritual sloth. Despair can disquiet our soul, make us fearful or lazy, and negatively affect our judgment. It can sap our strength and rob us of resolution. St. Francis likens despair to "a hard winter which takes away all the beauty from the earth ... for it takes away all sweetness from the soul, and makes her almost paralyzed and powerless" (4, 12).[99] All this can make us adverse to praying, but praying is just what St. Francis says we need to do.

"Is anyone among you suffering?" St. James writes in his epistle. "He should pray" (James 5:13). St. Francis says even though we might pray "coldly, sadly, and without fervor," we should nevertheless persist, because prayer raises our hearts and minds to God,

[99] Ross translation.

"who is our only joy and consolation." Even if our heart isn't in it, we should still go on, "for the enemy would fain enfeeble our good works by sadness, and when he finds that we will not discontinue them, and that they are all the more meritorious through resistance, he will cease to annoy us" (4, 12).

Practically speaking, St. Francis says, "It is also useful to be actively employed, and that with as much variety as may be, so as to divert the mind from the cause of its sadness" (4, 12). More practical advice is offered by none other than the Angelic Doctor, St. Thomas Aquinas. In the *Summa Theologiae*, he suggests countering sadness with pleasure, which may be derived from several legitimate means, including contemplating the truth in prayer or doing simple things such as resting, bathing, or just having a good cry.[100] "Just as repose of the body brings relief to weariness ...," St. Thomas writes, "pleasure brings relief to any kind of sorrow." So try watching a funny movie, having some ice cream, or taking a nice walk. The psalms teach us that wine gladdens the heart of man (Ps. 104:15). As long as it is not sinful, enjoying the good things of life can go a long way to getting us out of the doldrums.

St. Thomas Aquinas further suggests that sorrow can be lessened by sharing our burdens with a friend. Not only does this sharing lighten our load, but it reminds us that we are loved. St. Francis de Sales would agree. Whether we suffer from anxiety or sadness, he advises that we make known to our spiritual guide all our emotions and cares. "If you can disclose your anxiety to the guide of your soul, or at least to some pious and trustworthy friend, doubt not that you will be speedily relieved" (4, 11). Often when we are burdened with worry, what helps most is just to talk about it.

---

[100] *Summa Theologiae*, I–II, q. 38.

# The Devout Life

"Seek the society of devout persons," St. Francis writes, "and above all resign yourself into God's hands, disposing yourself to suffer your grievous sadness with patience ... and never doubt that when God has sufficiently tried you, He will set you free from this trial" (4, 12).

## Questions for Reflection

1.  Has there been a time when enduring sorrow with patience and gentleness has brought you closer to God?
2.  What do you do to help alleviate your sorrows? Does prayer play a role in helping you to overcome worry or sadness?
3.  In thinking about the causes of your sorrows, are you able to identify any that would lead you to repentance or to change patterns of behavior?

## Scripture for Meditation

Have no anxiety at all, but in everything, by prayer and petition, with thanksgiving, make your requests known to God. Then the peace of God that surpasses all understanding will guard your hearts and minds. (Phil. 4:6–7)

# 5

# Consolation

Just as day leads into night, and every summer turns into winter and then to summer again, man also has his seasons. We live in a transitory world, and no two days are alike. As the author of Ecclesiastes says, "There is an appointed time for everything ... a time to weep, and a time to laugh; a time to mourn, and a time to dance" (Eccles. 3:1, 4).

In the midst of this ever-changing world, our goal should be to maintain an evenness of spirit. "Although all things around us change and vary," St. Francis de Sales writes, "we must ever remain content and unmoved in looking, seeking, and longing after our God." He likens the soul to a ship tossed about by a storm at sea. As long as her compass points north, she will remain on course. Our soul's compass, which he says is "our heart, our mind, and our superior will ... must ceaselessly and perpetually tend to the love of God.... This absolute resolution never to forsake God, or leave His tender love, serves to balance our souls, and preserve them in holy evenness, amidst the unevenness of this life's restless motion" (4, 13).

It is this resolution toward God that is the heart of devotion, whatever outward feelings or affections we may experience. This general principle is important to keep in mind as we consider the topic of spiritual *consolation* and *desolation*. These two terms have been popularized in the Church in large part due to the role they play in the *Spiritual Exercises* of St. Ignatius of Loyola.

There is a temptation to oversimplify things by equating consolation with "good feelings" and desolation with "bad feelings." There is more to it than that. St. Ignatius describes what he means by *consolation*:

> I call it consolation when some interior movement of the soul is caused, through which the soul comes to be inflamed with love of its Creator and Lord.... Likewise, when it sheds tears that move to love of its Lord, whether out of sorrow for one's sins, or for the Passion of Christ our Lord, or because of other things directly connected with His service and praise. Finally, I call consolation every increase of hope, faith and charity, and all interior joy which calls and attracts to heavenly things and to the salvation of one's soul, quieting it and giving it peace in its Creator and Lord.[101]

Thus, consolation is more about the peace and interior joy our soul experiences that stems from a true love of God, which may manifest itself in either laughter or tears. We may experience moments of consolation in prayer, but we won't always. St. Francis offers points to keep in mind when considering the consolations we may or may not experience.

This first is not to mistake consolation for devotion. "Devotion does not consist in that sweetness, consolation, and visible tenderness, which provokes tears and sighs, and gives us a certain agreeable savor and satisfaction in our spiritual exercises." There are some who experience great consolation in prayer. Their hearts are easily moved to compassion for our Lord by looking upon a crucifix, for example. It is good to find joy in thinking about holy things. But devotion consists of "a constant, resolute, prompt, and

---

[101] St. Ignatius of Loyola, *Spiritual Exercises*, pt. 2, chap. 6.

active will to execute what we know to be pleasing to God" (4, 13). Someone who feels very close to God during moments of prayer but lives otherwise with little thought of God or charitable concern for neighbor is not truly devout. Another may rarely or never experience consolation during prayer but nevertheless remains resolute to do God's will for the love of God. Such a person is truly devout.

The second point St. Francis makes is that, although consolations are not to be equated with devotion, they can be very good and useful for devotion. Consolations can "excite the soul's appetite, comfort the mind, and add to the earnestness of devotion a holy joy and gladness" (4, 13). They can make all our spiritual exercises more agreeable and should be considered gifts from God. "Such heavenly consolations are as foretastes of the eternity of bliss which God gives to those souls who seek it," St. Francis writes. "They resemble the sugared bribes we give to children; they are as cordial waters given by God to comfort the soul, and sometimes they are the pledges of everlasting rewards" (4, 13).

We offer children "sugared bribes," as St. Francis calls them, to make it easier for them to endure things that may be unpleasant but are necessary. I remember accompanying my father to the bank when I was young enough to sit on the teller's counter while my father did his business. There is not much in a bank to interest a child, but there was always a bowl of lollipops there to reward my patience. Similarly, our family dentist has a bin of small prizes that children can pick from after they've endured having their teeth cleaned. As Mary Poppins sings so eloquently, "A spoonful of sugar helps the medicine go down." God can and does offer His consolations at times to make the medicine He prescribes sweeter. The memory of past consolations can make future trials easier to bear, especially when we consider that they are but pale shadows of the joy we will know in Heaven.

But how are we to know the difference between true consolation of the Spirit and good or comforting emotions we may naturally experience? This is St. Francis's third point to consider. Once, at the beginning of a silent retreat, I sat down in the chapel of the retreat house to pray and was overwhelmed by an immediate sense of peace. Was that a consolation from the Holy Spirit or merely my mind and body relaxing due to being away from my usual daily concerns? (I thanked God for it, in any case). St. Francis de Sales says, "The general rule concerning the passions and emotions of our souls is that we should know them by their fruits; our hearts are as trees, our affections and passions are the branches, and their actions and deeds are the fruit" (4, 13). If the consolations we receive lead to us become more humble, charitable, patient, compassionate, or obedient, they are bearing good and holy fruit and are of the Spirit. If they make us more proud, impatient, or obstinate, then they are what St. Francis calls "false consolations."

Consolations may lead to us become proud or presumptuous if we mistakenly believe that we are holy because we receive them. As I mentioned above, someone with a sensitive spirit may be easily moved to tears of compassion by gazing upon our crucified Lord. If he mistakes his natural emotions for devotion, he may believe himself to be already holy and so neglect his necessary spiritual growth. This can be true even if the compassion he feels is a special consolation from God. St. Francis's fourth consideration is a warning not to value the gift over the Giver.

"If we enjoy much sweetness and consolation," he writes, "we must humble ourselves profoundly before God, and beware saying on account of such favors, 'How good I am!' ... Let us rather say, 'Oh, how good God is to those who love Him'" (4, 13). If God gives us good things, it is because God is good, not because we are good. "No one is good but God alone" (Mark 10:18). We should therefore accept in humility whatever consolations we receive, knowing that we don't deserve them (that's what makes them gifts!), thanking God for them in our hearts, and disposing ourselves to use them for God's purposes.

God gives us the consolations we need, and when He doesn't give consolations, it is because He wants us to seek Him and not His gifts. When I wait in line at the bank now, I don't take a lollipop from the bowl (usually), because I know how to be patient without it. St. Francis's final point regarding consolations is that, good though they may be,

> it is not such gratifications that we seek, but God and His holy love; not the comfort, but the Comforter; not the sweetness, but the most sweet Savior; not the delight itself, but Him who is the delight of Heaven and earth; and with such feelings we should dispose ourselves to abide steadfast in His holy love, even though our life long we were to know no consolation; willing always to say, "Lord, it is good to be where Thou art, in glory or in agony," be it on Mount Calvary or on Mount Tabor. (4, 13)

1. Have you experienced consolation in prayer? Do you think that it helped strengthen you for later trials?
2. How do you distinguish between spiritual consolation and natural emotions or affections?
3. If you have not experienced consolation (or haven't for quite some time), what effect does this have on your practice of devotion?

*Scripture for Meditation*

What will separate us from the love of Christ? Will anguish, or distress, or persecution, or famine, or nakedness, or peril, or the sword?... No, in all these things we conquer overwhelmingly through him who loved us. For I am convinced that neither death, nor life, nor angels, nor principalities, nor present things, nor future things, nor powers, nor height, nor depth, nor any other creature will be able to separate us from the love of God in Christ Jesus our Lord. (Rom. 8:35, 37–39)

How sweet to my tongue is your promise, sweeter than honey to my mouth! (Ps. 119:103)

6

# Spiritual Dryness

As mentioned in the previous chapter, God does not always grant consolations to those who seek Him, and it is quite common to experience times of desolation, or spiritual dryness. These feelings of dryness in prayer and in the service of God may be brief or may persist for quite some time and can be a cause of great distress to those who think that God has abandoned them. Such feelings may lead to doubts about God's love or His very existence. We therefore need to be on guard against the temptations that can arise from spiritual dryness, as we are often quite unable to prevent the dryness itself. In fact, sometimes it can be a gift from God.

St. Francis recognizes that feelings of dryness may arise for a variety of reasons, some of which can be purely physical. "Sometimes disinclination, dryness, and barrenness of heart proceed from bodily indisposition," he writes. If we have been working too hard, or not eating or sleeping well, our bodily exhaustion can affect our minds and spirits, as these things are related. St. Francis says, "The fitting remedy in such a case is to reinvigorate the body by means of some lawful relaxation and recreation" (4, 15). Take a break. Relax. Eat well and get to bed on time. Take a few days off from work for a retreat. You may find you have more vigor for prayer and spiritual exercises once your body has been renewed. The benefits of going on a retreat arise not only from the spiritual counsels you may receive but also from the physical and mental relaxation that comes from escaping your ordinary duties for a while.

Spiritual dryness cannot always be attributed to physical exhaustion, however. Feelings of desolation may result from spiritual negligence. St. Francis says, "We ourselves are often the cause of our own dryness and barrenness." He suggests several faults that can lead to dryness if we allow them to persist: if we have become complacent in our faith, if we have been dishonest or unforthright with our confessor or spiritual director, if we have become too attached to the consolations of this world or indeed too attached to the consolations that come from God. For any of these reasons, God might remove His consolations from us, for our own good. If you experience spiritual dryness, St. Francis says, "carefully examine your conscience, and see whether you discover any such faults" (4, 14). If you do, then be thankful, for that means the remedy is close at hand.

But spiritual dryness often occurs for no discernable reason. In that case, here is how St. Francis would advise us to proceed. First, in prayer, "humble yourself profoundly before God." Acknowledge that you are nothing without Him and completely in need of Him.

Second, call upon God to restore gladness to your soul. You can use the words of the psalmist: "Restore to me the gladness of your salvation" (Ps. 51:14) or simply express your desire in your own words.

Third, make a good confession. Review in the first section of this book the meditations and guidance on making a devotional confession. Listen carefully to your confessor's advice, for as St. Francis observes, God "often blesses the advice we receive from others, especially from the guides of souls, even when such a result appears but unlikely" (4, 14).

Fourth, try not to be overeager in your desire to be delivered from your dryness. Although it is good to want your dryness to end, do not grow impatient. It is better to desire God's will, even if God's will is that you experience spiritual dryness for the time being. St. Francis says that if we make Jesus' prayer our own, "Father, if you are willing, take this cup away from me," we should not forget to add, "still, not my will but yours be done" (Luke 22:42). Place yourself in the hands of God's providence and there find rest. Pray in the words of Job: "The LORD gave and the LORD has taken away: blessed be the name of the LORD" (Job 1:21).

Finally, St. Francis says to have courage and persist in prayer and good works, even if you fail to receive consolation from them. In fact, he suggests that you increase your prayer and good works, if you are able. "If we cannot bring fresh fruits to our Beloved, let us at least offer those that are dry; for to Him all are the same, so long as they are offered by a heart wholly resolved to love Him" (4, 14).

We may feel that if our service to God is less pleasing to us, it is somehow less pleasing to God. This is absolutely not true. St. Francis writes, "Although those works which we perform with a kindled heart are more agreeable to us, who consider only our own gratification, yet, if they are performed amidst drought and barrenness, they are more costly and fragrant unto God" (4, 14). He offers the example of placing yourself in the service of a great prince. There is little merit in serving him amid the pleasures of the court in times of peace and tranquility. But if you are willing to serve him during times of war and trial, that is a mark of great loyalty and faithfulness. God sees and recognizes when we persist in our prayer and good deeds even though it is a struggle and we find no personal pleasure in doing them. He knows, then, that we do so purely out of love for Him and not for our own benefit.

No saint in history has more experience with spiritual dryness than St. John of the Cross, and no saint in modern times has experienced it more than St. Teresa of Calcutta. In the spiritual classic *Dark Night of the Soul*, St. John of the Cross considers spiritual dryness as an invitation to "purgative contemplation" and a necessary stage in growing to spiritual maturity. He compares it to a mother weaning her child. "God ... weans them from the breasts that they may become strong, and cast their swaddling-clothes aside: He carries them in His arms no longer, and shows them how to walk alone."[102] Times of dryness are invitations from God to love Him for His own sake and not for the gifts He gives us. St. John writes, "God leads into the dark night those whom He desires to purify from all these imperfections so that He may bring them farther onward."[103] Similarly, St. Francis de Sales observes that "by these trials God would lead us to great purity of heart, to entire renunciation of our own interest where His service is concerned, and to a perfect setting aside of self" (4, 15).

Until a collection of her personal correspondence was published in 2007, most people never suspected that Mother Teresa, the little Albanian nun who dedicated her life to caring for the poorest of the poor on the streets of Calcutta, experienced her own "dark night" that lasted fifty years. In *Come Be My Light*, it was revealed that once she answered the call to found the Missionaries of Charity, which she did as a total surrender to God's will, she ceased finding any consolation in prayer. This pained her greatly, as she felt God was absent from her life. This admission caused many of her detractors to gleefully accuse her of hypocrisy and unbelief, "just making a show" of all her piety. What they failed to understand is that Mother Teresa remained faithful to her ministry

---

[102] St. John of the Cross, *Dark Night of the Soul*, trans. David Lewis (Charlotte, NC: TAN Books, 2010), bk. 1, chap. 8.

[103] St. John of the Cross, *Dark Night of the Soul*, bk. 1, chap. 2.

for all those years without consolation purely for the love of God. Her persistence amid desolation is a sign of her great faith.

Ultimately Mother Teresa came to recognize her long, dark night as connected to her promise to surrender her will completely to God. God was allowing her to experience the abandonment that Jesus felt on the Cross: "My God, my God, why have you forsaken me?" (Matt. 27:46). That prayer was Mother Teresa's for fifty years. But God did not forsake her, any more than He forsook Jesus. St. Teresa's willingness to accept her dryness for the love of God was her share of the Passion of Christ.

Prior to the start of her missionary work in 1949, Teresa received many consolations from God in prayer. These sweet memories served to sustain her faith during her long decades of dryness. So St. Francis de Sales encourages us to "carefully preserve the fruit of past consolations" (4, 14). The memories of them can be a sweet balm to our spirit long after the consolation itself has ended.

Whether our times of dryness are long or short, frequent or infrequent, we can take comfort in the knowledge that God grants us both the consolation and the desolation that we need, and He works all things for the good of those who love Him (Rom. 8:28).

## Questions for Reflection

1. Have you experienced times of dryness in your spiritual life? Has it tempted you to abandon your duty to prayer and devotion?
2. St. Francis mentions that spiritual dryness can sometimes be our own fault. What things of our own doing might lead to feelings of distance from God?
3. What does it mean for us to know that great saints such as St. John of the Cross and St. Teresa of Calcutta experienced profound desolation?

## Scripture for Meditation

My God, my God, why have you abandoned me?
Why so far from my call for help,
from my cries of anguish?
My God, I call by day, but you do not answer;
by night, but I have no relief.
Yet you are enthroned as the Holy One;
you are the glory of Israel. (Ps. 22:2–4)

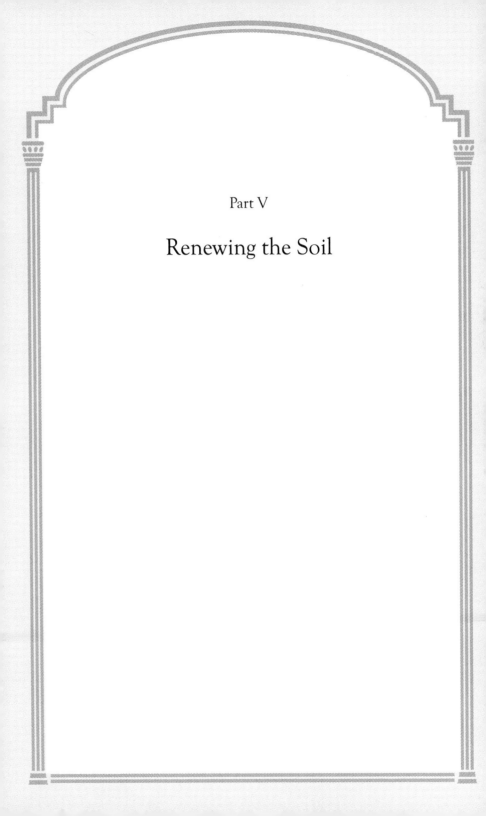

Part V

# Renewing the Soil

1

# Making an Annual Retreat

Canon law encourages priests both to take vacations[104] and to make retreats[105] because these two things are quite different. Getting away from parish life for a few days and kicking one's heels up at the beach can be a necessary preventative against pastoral burnout, but it is not a spiritual retreat. And while a retreat can indeed leave one feeling refreshed and renewed, it is not a vacation. Indeed, it is a time of work—the deep, spiritual work that can be difficult to focus on in the midst of one's ordinary daily obligations.

Annual retreats are expected for clergy because of their spiritual responsibilities in the Church, but the practice is strongly recommended for any lay Catholic. We all have a need to examine our lives and renew our faith from time to time, and it can be difficult to find the time to dig into this deep work amid our daily duties.

St. Francis de Sales likens our spiritual lives to a clock. Even the best clock needs to be wound daily (he wrote before the age of digital clocks and batteries). And so we have our daily means of "winding up" our faith: our regular devotion to prayer, spiritual reading, and participation in the sacraments, as outlined in part 2 of this book.

But if you want to maintain the clock in good order, St. Francis says, once a year you have to take it completely apart. You need to

---

[104] CIC 533§2.
[105] CIC 276§2 n. 4.

remove all its pieces, clean them, remove any rust, examine them to make sure they are in good order, oil them, and put the whole thing back together again, making sure everything is in balance. Maybe you've never done maintenance on a clock (you might not even own one that you need to wind by hand). But consider your routine car maintenance. You have to fill it up with gas, keep air in the tires, and change the oil every three thousand miles, just to keep it running. But once a year you also need to take it in for an inspection. Or think of your own body. It's important to exercise, eat well, and get good sleep to maintain your health. But even if you do those things every day, you should still have an annual physical, just to make sure nothing is out of order. Your soul needs an occasional tune-up, too, like a clock or a car. You wouldn't call it an annual "physical" but an annual "spiritual." That's the purpose of a retreat.

"He who takes good care of his heart," St. Francis writes, "will wind it up towards God night and morning.... Besides this, he will from time to time examine into his condition, correct and regulate it; and at least once a year he will take it to pieces and examine all its parts in detail, that is to say, all its affections and passions, in order to correct their defects" (5, 1).

For this purpose, St. Francis provides a series of examinations and considerations to reflect on using the method of mental prayer outlined in part 2 of this book. We will go over these in the following pages. Here I wish to share a few words about making a retreat in general.

There are today a great variety of Catholic retreats on offer—some at retreat centers, others at local parishes. Some offer on-site accommodations, and others require you to arrange your own lodging. Some are silent, and others encourage group discussions. Most are led by retreat masters who present talks on a theme and perhaps offer on-site spiritual guidance. All of these are good but are not necessarily the kind of retreat St. Francis has in mind (though, depending on the nature of the talks, they can serve the same purpose, assuming they allow time for sufficient personal reflection).

In order that we may devote time to the spiritual exercises St. Francis provides, our retreat should consist mainly of silent time for individual prayer and reflection. If it allows for the opportunity to attend Mass and go to Confession, all the better. A dedicated Catholic retreat center will have an on-site chapel for prayer and adoration before the Blessed Sacrament. But if there is not such a facility near you, renting a cabin or even staying in a hotel room can provide you with sufficient quiet time away to perform these exercises, and it should not be too hard to find one close to a Catholic parish so you can participate in the sacraments.

It is possible even to do an at-home retreat if you are not able to get away, although this comes with its own challenges. It can be difficult to step away from our daily routine in our own homes, and if you live with family, finding quiet time may be a challenge. Do your best in this case to allocate time during the day to devote a few hours to prayer and reflection. Let your family know what you are doing, so they will respect the time you need to be alone in your room or wherever you are seeking solitude.

Another advantage of retreat centers is that they generally have staff on hand to provide meals and other necessities, so you do not have to concern yourself with those things. If you are doing an at-home retreat, try to minimize any other work you must do. Make your meals in advance, order food to be delivered, or ask another family member to prepare meals. The point is to give yourself time away from your daily chores to focus on spiritual work.

Whether you make your retreat at home or at another facility, don't hesitate to stretch your legs and go for a walk. Not all of the reflection St. Francis asks us to do requires us to be on our knees in deep prayer. In fact, it is best to take things slowly and to allow time for more passive reflection, ruminating on the fruits of our more intense spiritual exercises.

Now go back and reread the chapters in part 2 on prayer—especially chapter 3, on meditation—as well as part 1, chapter 6. We will be following a similar method of meditation for the exercises to follow. The first four meditations serve as an examination of conscience and should be followed as soon as possible by a good confession. The remaining five meditations are reflections meant to inspire your devotion to God and encourage you in His service.

You don't want to rush through these meditations, but neither should you space them too far apart. The beauty of a retreat is that you have the time dedicated to prayer and reflection. If you are making your retreat at home and still have other duties to attend to, try to do at least two meditations a day (one in the morning and one in the evening), or three, if possible. If you are able to get away, you should be able to make your way through three or four in a day, but do not try to do more than that. You don't want your meditations to be laborious, and your mind needs time to rest and ruminate on the affections and resolutions from each meditation.

*Questions for Reflection*

1. How would you describe the difference between a retreat and a vacation? When (if ever) was the last retreat you made?
2. Are you aware of any Catholic retreat centers near you? Are there local parishes that offer retreats? Where else might you consider going on a personal retreat?
3. If planning a retreat at home, what are some considerations or preparations you would need to make to get the most out of your experience?

*Scripture for Meditation*

The apostles gathered together with Jesus and reported all they had done and taught. He said to them, "Come away by yourselves to a deserted place and rest a while." People were coming and going in great numbers, and they had no opportunity even to eat. So they went off in the boat by themselves to a deserted place. (Mark 6:30–32)

## Meditation 1: Your Pledge of Devotion

*Preparation*

1. Place yourself in the presence of God.
2. Ask the Holy Spirit to inspire your prayer: "Lord, teach me to know You and to know myself."

*Considerations*

1. Remember the renewal of baptismal promises you made when you first pledged your devotion to God.[106] You renounced all mortal sin; you dedicated every part of your being to serving God; and you promised that should you again fall into sin you would not hesitate to rise again, with God's help, and seek His mercy.
2. Consider that you made this pledge to God. If we are bound by our promises to men, how much more are we bound by our promises to God?
3. Consider that you made this pledge in the presence of Jesus Christ, His Immaculate Mother, St. Joseph, and all the angels and saints, with joy in Heaven at your pledge of devotion.
4. Consider how God drew you to Himself through prayer, the sacraments, and spiritual reading, and what consolations He has given you.

---

[106] See pt. I, chap. 7.

5. Consider your life before you began the practice of devotion and what has changed for you since then.

*Affections and Resolutions*

1. Humble yourself before God. Pray with St. Augustine: "Too late have I loved you, O Beauty so ancient, O Beauty so new, too late have I loved you!"[107]
2. Give God glory for any progress you have made.
3. Resolve to correct, with God's grace, any faults you uncover during the following meditations.

*Conclusion*

1. Give thanks to God.
2. Pray: *Our Father... Hail Mary... Glory be...*
3. Reflect on your time of prayer and make a spiritual nosegay.

---

[107] St. Augustine, *Confessions*, bk. 10, chap. 27.

## MEDITATION 2: YOUR RELATIONSHIP WITH GOD

*Preparation*

1. Place yourself in the presence of God.
2. Ask the Holy Spirit to inspire your prayer: "Lord, teach me to know You and to know myself."

*Considerations*

1. What is the state of your heart regarding God's commandments? Do you find them light or burdensome? Are there particular sins, even venial ones, to which you are especially inclined?
2. What is the state of your heart regarding your spiritual exercises: prayer, meditation, spiritual reading, the sacraments (especially Confession and the Eucharist), and the practice of virtue? Do you find them pleasant or burdensome? If there are those you are disinclined to, what is the cause of that?
3. What is the state of your heart toward God? Do you delight in thinking of Him? Do you seek repose in God amid your daily occupations and concerns? Do you speak of God fondly and delight in praising Him?
4. Have you developed a devotion to the Blessed Mother, your guardian angel, and the saints? Do you delight in thinking of the lives of holy people?

5. Do you seek to glorify God by your good works?
6. Have you renounced anything for God's sake?

*Affections and Resolutions*

1. Humble yourself before God.
2. Give God glory for any progress you have made.
3. Resolve to correct, with God's grace, any faults you uncover. Note where you have fallen short so that you may confess them and receive spiritual counsel.

*Conclusion*

1. Give thanks to God.
2. Pray: *Our Father... Hail Mary... Glory be...*
3. Reflect on your time of prayer and make a spiritual nosegay.

## MEDITATION 3: YOUR RELATIONSHIP WITH YOURSELF

*Preparation*

1. Place yourself in the presence of God.
2. Ask the Holy Spirit to inspire your prayer: "Lord, teach me to know You and to know myself."

*Considerations*

1. Think about what occupies your mind. Are your concerns primarily for this world? Or are your concerns also for heavenly things?
2. Is your love of self properly regulated? Do you intentionally strive to increase in virtue and decrease in vice? Are you concerned more for the opinion of God or the opinion of men?
3. Are you conscious of the need to love your soul and care for its spiritual health?
4. How do you see yourself in the light of God?
5. Are you humble not only before God but before other people? Do you desire to be esteemed or praised? Do you seek to increase others' opinion of yourself by boasting or flattery?
6. How do you spend your time? Do you dutifully attend to the obligations and responsibilities proper to your vocation and state of life for the love of God? Do you spend your recreational or leisure

time engaging in anything that may be harmful to your soul?

*Affections and Resolutions*

1.  Humble yourself before God.
2.  Give God glory for any progress you have made.
3.  Resolve to correct, with God's grace, any faults you uncover. Note where you have fallen short so that you may confess them and receive spiritual counsel.

*Conclusion*

1.  Give thanks to God.
2.  Pray: *Our Father... Hail Mary... Glory be...*
3.  Reflect on your time of prayer and make a spiritual nosegay.

## Meditation 4: Your Relationship with Your Neighbor

*Preparation*

1. Place yourself in the presence of God.
2. Ask the Holy Spirit to inspire your prayer: "Lord, teach me to know You and to know myself."

*Considerations*

1. Who is neighbor to you? To whom in your life do you owe special obligations? Are you married? Do you have children? Aging parents? Consider friends, co-workers, parishioners at your church, and members of your community. What love and service do you owe them?
2. What is the state of your heart toward those people? Do you love them for the sake of God? Do you recognize each one to be someone made in God's image, for whom God's Son gave His life on the Cross?
3. Think of those whom you find to be disagreeable or troublesome. What is the state of your heart toward them? Do you love them for the sake of God, or do you find that to be a challenge?
4. How do you speak of others, in private or in public? Is it always with the respect and reverence they deserve as children of God?

5. Have you caused injury to your neighbor, either directly or through negligence, by not giving what assistance you could in his or her time of need?
6. Can you truly say that you consider your neighbor as "another self"?

*Affections and Resolutions*

1. Humble yourself before God.
2. Give God glory for any progress you have made.
3. Resolve to correct, with God's grace, any faults you uncover. Note where you have fallen short so that you may confess them and receive spiritual counsel.

*Conclusion*

1. Give thanks to God.
2. Pray: *Our Father... Hail Mary... Glory be...*
3. Reflect on your time of prayer and make a spiritual nosegay.

## MEDITATION 5: THE EXCELLENCE OF THE SOUL

*Preparation*

1. Place yourself in the presence of God.
2. Ask the Holy Spirit to inspire your prayer: "Lord, teach me to know You and to know myself."

*Considerations*

1. Consider the nobility of the human soul. God has made us "little less than a god" (Ps. 8:6), with the capacity to know not only earthly things but also heavenly things and, indeed, to know God Himself.
2. Consider that your soul has the capacity not only to know God but to love Him and that indeed your heart cannot find rest except in God. Think of all the things you have sought to find satisfaction in before and how inadequate they were.
3. Consider that you were made to serve God and not any other creature, and that since this is why God made you, God will doubtless give you the grace to do so.

*Affections and Resolutions*

1. Humble yourself before God.
2. Say to yourself: "O my soul, you are able to know, love, and serve God. Why, then, take pleasure in

anything short of Him? You can aim at eternity. Why trifle away your energy on temporary things?"

3. Since your soul is capable of knowing God and indeed will not find rest without Him, resolve not to be satisfied with anything less.

*Conclusion*

1. Give thanks to God.
2. Renew your dedication to His service and ask Him to grant you strength to serve Him well.
3. Pray: *Our Father... Hail Mary... Glory be...*
4. Reflect on your time of prayer and make a spiritual nosegay.

## Meditation 6: The Excellence of Virtue

*Preparation*

1. Place yourself in the presence of God.
2. Ask the Holy Spirit to inspire your prayer: "Lord, teach me to know You and to know myself."

*Considerations*

1. Consider the meaning of *virtue*. Virtues are the qualities of goodness in a human person. Consider that to be a good person is to be more authentically what God made you to be.
2. Consider that only virtue (being your true, good self) and devotion (loving and serving God) can satisfy your soul in this world.
3. Consider how beautiful, good, and true the virtues are compared with their opposing vices: patience compared with revenge, gentleness compared with anger, humility compared with pride and ambition, generosity compared with greed, charity compared with envy, temperance compared to gluttony and indulgence.
4. Consider how your soul feels after practicing acts of virtue, compared with the state of your soul after committing acts of vice.

*Affections and Resolutions*

1. Humble yourself before God.
2. Thank God for any advancement you have made in virtue.
3. Ask God to strengthen you against any temptations to vice.

*Conclusion*

1. Give thanks to God.
2. Pray: *Our Father... Hail Mary... Glory be...*
3. Reflect on your time of prayer and make a spiritual nosegay.

## Meditation 7: The Excellence of the Saints

*Preparation*

1. Place yourself in the presence of God.
2. Ask the Holy Spirit to inspire your prayer: "Lord, teach me to know You and to know myself."

*Considerations*

1. Consider the example of the saints. Consider how their lives exemplify what it means to be a servant of God, in all its variety and splendor, through all the trials and circumstances of this life.
2. Consider the martyrs and how steadfast they were in their faith. Consider all that they suffered for the love of God.
3. Consider the holy virgin martyrs who, even as young girls, gave themselves so fully to the love of God that they did not hold back from offering even their lives, so constant was their faith.
4. Consider the holy confessors, those who suffered a white martyrdom by living their lives already dead to the pleasures of this world so that they might more freely and willingly embrace the joy and peace that Heaven has to offer.
5. Consider the saints who found holiness in matrimony, serving God by giving themselves in service to their families and witnessing by the love shown

to their spouses the love that exists between Christ
and His Bride, the Church.

*Affections and Resolutions*

1. Humble yourself before God.
2. Resolve to follow the example of the saints. They
   were what we are. They served the same God, to attain the same graces. There is no reason we cannot
   do the same, according to our own circumstances
   and vocations.
3. Pray that God grants you the strength and resolve
   to be a saint.

*Conclusion*

1. Give thanks to God.
2. Pray: *Our Father... Hail Mary... Glory be...*
3. Reflect on your time of prayer and make a spiritual
   nosegay.

## MEDITATION 8: THE EXCELLENCE OF CHRIST'S LOVE

*Preparation*

1. Place yourself in the presence of God.
2. Ask the Holy Spirit to inspire your prayer: "Lord, teach me to know You and to know myself."

*Considerations*

1. Consider the love that Jesus Christ bore for us in His sufferings.
2. Consider that all His sufferings and trials were for you, to obtain for you the grace needed to be with Him, to serve Him in this life, and to love Him forever in eternity.
3. Consider that Christ's love obtained for you every good you will ever possess.
4. Consider that before you were even born, Christ knew you and loved you. "Before I formed you in the womb I knew you, before you were born I dedicated you" (Jer. 1:5).
5. Consider that Christ has given you all the necessary means of salvation.
6. Consider that Christ is calling you even now to come closer to Him.

7. Consider how Christ has arranged all the circumstances of your life to bring you to this moment, to love Him.

*Affections and Resolutions*

1. Humble yourself before God.
2. Engrave upon your soul the thought that Christ loves you and did all these things for you as though you were His only beloved one.
3. Resolve firmly to love Him always in return.

*Conclusion*

1. Give thanks to God.
2. Pray: *Our Father... Hail Mary... Glory be...*
3. Reflect on your time of prayer and make a spiritual nosegay.

## MEDITATION 9: THE EXCELLENCE OF GOD'S LOVE

*Preparation*

1. Place yourself in the presence of God.
2. Ask the Holy Spirit to inspire your prayer: "Lord, teach me to know You and to know myself."

*Considerations*

1. Consider the eternal love of God. Even before He sent His Son into the world to suffer and die for you, God knew you and loved you exceedingly.
2. "When did God begin to love you?" St. Francis asks. He answers, "When He began to be God. And when was His beginning? Never, for He has always been, without beginning and without end" (5, 14). Such is God's eternal love for you. "With age-old love I have loved you" (Jer. 31:3).
3. Consider God's eternal sovereignty, and that every act of God in your life has been and will always be an act of love. God is completely and eternally resolved to love you.

*Affections and Resolutions*

1. Humble yourself before the love of God.
2. God's will and His love are strong and eternal. Our human will and our love are weak and fickle. Resolve to love God always and ask for His strength

to help you in this resolution each day, so that His love will not fail to bear fruit in your life.

*Conclusion*

1. Give thanks to God.
2. Pray: *Our Father... Hail Mary... Glory be...*
3. Reflect on your time of prayer and make a spiritual nosegay.

## 2

# The Conclusion of These Exercises

After having prayerfully gone through the previous meditations, carefully consider all of the resolutions you have made and renewed in your heart. These resolutions will keep you on the path toward Heaven, for they are your soul's cooperation and commitment to God's grace. St. Francis offers this touching reflection upon them.

> O cherished resolutions! You are as the tree of life which God has with his own hand planted in the midst of my heart, and which my Savior waters with his own blood that it may bring forth fruit. Rather would I die a thousand deaths than suffer any blast of wind to uproot you. No, neither vanity nor pleasure, neither poverty nor wealth shall ever alter my intentions.... Good and holy resolutions I will keep you, and you shall keep me: if you live in my soul, my soul will live in you. Live forever then, O good resolutions! (5, 15)

At the conclusion of these exercises, make note of whatever may be necessary to aid you in maintaining these resolutions. Consider your daily commitment to prayer, your participation in the sacraments, and your works of charity. Consider any faults that have been uncovered through these exercises and commit to amending them with the help of your spiritual director. Resolve to avoid near occasions of sin that may lead you into avoidable temptation. Speak with your spiritual director about these things and follow his counsels. Make another general confession (see part 1, chapter 7). Then receive Holy Communion and recommit yourself to God with renewed vigor and vitality.

The most important day of any spiritual retreat is the day after it ends. As lovely as it is to have this time dedicated to renewing our devotion to God, you must enter back into the world and return to your daily occupations. But though you return to the world, you are no longer a citizen of the world. You belong to Christ. St. Francis prays, "I am no more my own, whether I live or die I am my Savior's! There is no more any 'I' or 'mine' – 'I' am Christ's – 'mine' is to be his" (5, 16). Let this thought sink into your heart and saturate your very being, so that your everyday routine will be filled with an everyday holiness. Devotion is no more to be practiced only on special days of retreat than prayer is to be practiced only on one's knees in a church. The purpose of these dedicated times is to infuse all time with the grace and the love of God.

## Questions for Reflection

1. Having made your annual retreat, what key resolutions did you make? Did your reflections go as expected, or did they uncover anything that surprised you?

2. What challenges do you anticipate in keeping the resolutions you made on this retreat once you return to your daily life? What things might you do to mitigate those challenges?

3. If this is not your first retreat, how did this experience compare with other retreats you have been on? You might consider writing down key affections and resolutions from this retreat to revisit during later retreats as a means of tracking your spiritual progress.

## Scripture for Meditation

I have been crucified with Christ; yet I live, no longer I, but Christ lives in me; insofar as I now live in the flesh, I live by faith in the Son of God who has loved me and given himself up for me. (Gal. 2:19–20)

3

# Some Parting Advice

After reading to the end of this book, some may be thinking, "This is all too much. I want to be a more devout Christian, but if I were to do all of this, I wouldn't have time for anything else. It's not realistic." St. Francis de Sales answers this objection: "If it were needful to perform all these exercises every day, undoubtedly they would wholly engross us, but they are required only at certain times and places, according to our circumstances" (5, 17). In other words, you don't need to do everything all at once. Do what you can.

The instructions offered throughout this text are not rules but recommendations to help us achieve the goal of holiness—the one worthwhile thing any of us can do in this life and, at the end of our lives, the only thing that will really matter. If you follow this guidance carefully, it is true you may find that there are things in your life that you no longer have time for because they serve only to distract you from your pursuit of holiness. On the other hand, the things of life that are truly good and worthy will be made sweeter and more fruitful by the practice of devotion.

St. Francis offers the example of St. Louis of France, who as king had many cares and obligations on his plate. Yet he attended daily Mass, prayed Vespers and Compline each day with his chaplain, devoted time to daily meditation, practiced mortification, and visited the sick once per week, all without neglecting his duties as king. In fact, France flourished under his reign. Mother Teresa's

Missionaries of Charity are able to do so much good work for the poor precisely because they never neglect their duty of daily prayer. If we make time for God, He will make time for us to accomplish all that He wishes us to do; and what He wishes us to do most of all is to be holy. In a sermon on the Lord's Passion, Pope St. Leo the Great cautions that "the business of this life should not preoccupy us with its anxiety and pride, so that we no longer strive with all the love of our heart to be like our Redeemer, and to follow his example."[108]

Some of the exercises and advice in this book will be more helpful at certain times than at others. The important thing is to grow in holiness, and if you are able to do this without some or all of the means St. Francis suggests, then by all means do so! But most of us need all the help we can get.

One of the most admirable things about *An Introduction to the Devout Life* is its proven track record. For four hundred years, faithful men and women have found in its pages useful guidance for practically applying their faith in Jesus Christ to their everyday lives. I have found no other text that covers the same width and breadth of instruction written for the average person, and that is why I wanted to bring it into the twenty-first century. It is not a prayer book; it is a book that teaches us how to pray. It is not a theology text; it is a text that applies theology to daily life. It is not so much a rule of life but a way of life that can be adopted by every person and adapted to our individual circumstances.

If you were to join a monastery, you would have a built-in structure to shape your devotional practice. When and how you pray, work, study, and rest would all be determined for you. Time

---

[108] *Sermon 15*, quoted in the Office of Readings for Thursday of the Fourth week of Lent.

would be allotted in your schedule for each, so nothing essential would be neglected. The sacraments and spiritual direction would always be close at hand.

We all can't be monks, but we are all called to be devout. As we discussed in the first part of this book, devotion is for everyone because holiness is for everyone, which is why St. Francis wrote the *Introduction* for the average Christian rather than for the monk. We all need structure in our lives to help us grow in holiness. The guidance offered in these pages will allow us to create a "rule" for ourselves in the midst of the world to prevent us from becoming too worldly and to keep our minds and hearts focused on Heaven. Our personal rule should include things we practice daily, weekly, monthly, and annually and will need to be adjusted from time to time as our circumstances change. Remember that the word *disciple* means "student." To be a disciple is to be always learning, always growing, always becoming more like Christ our Teacher.

For the sake of review, I have distilled St. Francis's advice into these essential elements that should be part of any devout life:

1. *Corporate worship*: As members of the Body of Christ, we have a duty to worship together with the Body. Attend Mass at least on Sundays and on holy days of obligation; attend more frequently if you are able.

2. *Daily prayer*: Scripture says to "pray without ceasing" (1 Thess. 5:17). St. Francis teaches a practical method of mental prayer we can do every day. In addition, he encourages us to begin and end our day in prayer and to find other opportunities to raise our minds and hearts to God throughout the day.

3. *Daily study*: It is difficult to practice a Faith we are igno-rant of, just as it is difficult to love a God we don't know. Devout Christians should know at least the basics of

the Faith. St. Francis recommends devoting a little time each day to spiritual reading, including Scripture and the writings of the saints. (Pro tip: If you pray the Office of Readings from the Liturgy of the Hours, you get this built in).

4. *Participation in the sacraments*: Receive the Eucharist reverently, as frequently as you are able, and go to Confession on a regular schedule.
5. *Penance*: It's not just for Lent. The more penance you perform here, the less you'll need to endure in Purgatory.
6. *Charity*: "Love your neighbor" is a commandment, not a suggestion.
7. *Self-reflection & spiritual direction*: What are your chief vices? What virtues do you need to grow in? How are you doing in your relationship with God and neighbor? These questions should be a part of your regular, ongoing reflection. It can be difficult to see yourself clearly (and easy to fool yourself), so having a spiritual director is important. An annual retreat allows time for a more intensive spiritual inventory.

Your practice of devotion should involve each of these elements in some form or another. Don't think of it as a spiritual to-do list but the means by which you till the soil of your heart to make it a fertile ground for God to plant His seed and the method by which you tend that seed so that it can grow and bear fruit. The fruit born of a life of devotion is holiness. In other words, if devotion is like gardening, holiness is the harvest.

Like working the garden, the practice of devotion is both laborious and rewarding. There will be some days when you just don't want to do it. For those days, St. Francis offers this simple encouraging reflection. Look up to Heaven and know that there is nothing here on earth worth forsaking it. Look down to Hell and know that there is nothing here on earth worth going there. And finally look at the Cross and know that your trials are part of Christ's Passion and are for that reason made sweet.

We will let our spiritual guide have the last word: "Never be ashamed of the ordinary and necessary actions which conduct us toward the love of God" (5, 18).

## Questions for Reflection

1. Having reviewed the seven essential elements of devotion outlined here, do you think that you need to improve upon any of them? What sections of this book might you want to go back and review?
2. What does your personal rule of devotion look like? Are there aspects of it that you might need to change in response to your current circumstances or spiritual needs?
3. What is your motivation to continue the practice of devotion through difficult or trying times? What aspects of devotion do you find most challenging? Most rewarding?

## Scripture for Meditation

Finally, brothers, we earnestly ask and exhort you in the Lord Jesus that, as you received from us how you should conduct yourselves to please God—and as you are conducting yourselves—you do so even more. (1 Thess. 4:1)

For I, the Lord, am your God. You shall make and keep yourselves holy, because I am holy. (Lev. 11:44)

# Concluding Prayer

O God, who for the salvation of souls willed that the Bishop Saint Francis de Sales become all things to all, graciously grant that, following his example, we may always display the gentleness of your charity in the service of our neighbor. Through our Lord Jesus Christ, your Son, who lives and reigns with you in the unity of the Holy Spirit, God, for ever and ever.[109]

[109] *Roman Missal*, Collect for the memorial of St. Francis de Sales (January 24).

# Works Cited

Barnard, Leslie William. *St. Justin Martyr: The First and Second Apologies*. Vol. 56 of Ancient Christian Writers. New York: Paulist Press, 1997.

Boylan, Eugene. *Difficulties in Mental Prayer*. (1943). Princeton: Scepter Publishers, 1997.

*Catechism of the Catholic Church*. 2nd ed. Vatican: Libreria Editrice Vaticana, 2012.

de Sales, St. Francis. *Consoling Thoughts of St. Francis de Sales: On Trials of an Interior Life*. Compiled by Père Huguet. Charlotte, NC: TAN Books, 2013.

——. *Introduction to the Devout Life*. Translated and edited by Allan Ross (1924). London: Baronius Press, 2015.

——. *Introduction to the Devout Life*. Translated and edited by John K. Ryan (1950). New York: Doubleday, 2003.

——. *Philothea, or An Introduction to the Devout Life*. (1923). Charlotte, NC: TAN Books, 2010.

*Didache Bible (New American Bible, Revised Edition)*. Downers Grove, IL: Midwest Theological Forum, 2015.

Ephraim the Syrian. *Hymns and Homilies of St. Ephraim the Syrian*. N.p.: Veritatis Splendor Publications, 2012.

Ignatius of Antioch. *The Letters of Saint Ignatius the God-Bearer, Bishop of Antioch*. Zeeland, MI: Legacy Icons, 2017.

John Chrysostom. *On Marriage and Family Life*. Translated by Catherine P. Roth and David Anderson. Crestwood, NY: St. Vladimir's Seminary Press, 1986.

John of the Cross. *Dark Night of the Soul.* Translated by David Lewis. Charlotte, NC: TAN Books, 2010.

Kreeft, Peter J. *Catholic Christianity.* San Francisco: Ignatius Press, 2001.

Lawrence of the Resurrection. *The Practice of the Presence of God with Spiritual Maxims.* Grand Rapids: Spire Books, 1967.

Newman, John Henry. *Parochial and Plain Sermons.* (1891). San Francisco: Ignatius Press, 1997.

*The Second Vatican Council: The Four Constitutions.* Translated by the Catholic Truth Society. San Francisco: Ignatius Press, 2013.

Pius XI. Encyclical *Rerum Omnium Perturbationem.* January 26, 1923.

# About the Author

Deacon Matthew Newsome was ordained for the Diocese of Charlotte in 2018. He has served as the Catholic Campus Minister for the students of Western Carolina University since 2008. His articles have appeared in *This Rock* (now *Catholic Answers Magazine*), *Envoy*, and *The Deacon*, and he writes a monthly column for the *Catholic News Herald*. He holds an MA in theology from Holy Apostles College. He and his wife have seven children.

# Sophia Institute

Sophia Institute is a nonprofit institution that seeks to nurture the spiritual, moral, and cultural life of souls and to spread the gospel of Christ in conformity with the authentic teachings of the Roman Catholic Church.

Sophia Institute Press fulfills this mission by offering translations, reprints, and new publications that afford readers a rich source of the enduring wisdom of mankind.

Sophia Institute also operates the popular online resource CatholicExchange.com. *Catholic Exchange* provides world news from a Catholic perspective as well as daily devotionals and articles that will help readers to grow in holiness and live a life consistent with the teachings of the Church.

In 2013, Sophia Institute launched Sophia Institute for Teachers to renew and rebuild Catholic culture through service to Catholic education. With the goal of nurturing the spiritual, moral, and cultural life of souls, and an abiding respect for the role and work of teachers, we strive to provide materials and programs that are at once enlightening to the mind and ennobling to the heart; faithful and complete, as well as useful and practical.

Sophia Institute gratefully recognizes the Solidarity Association for preserving and encouraging the growth of our apostolate over the course of many years. Without their generous and timely support, this book would not be in your hands.

www.SophiaInstitute.com
www.CatholicExchange.com
www.SophiaInstituteforTeachers.org

Sophia Institute Press® is a registered trademark of Sophia Institute.
Sophia Institute is a tax-exempt institution as defined by the
Internal Revenue Code, Section 501(c)(3). Tax ID 22-2548708.